THE AGILITY ADVANTAGE

THE AGILITY ADVANTAGE

HOW TO IDENTIFY AND ACT ON OPPORTUNITIES IN A FAST-CHANGING WORLD

Amanda Setili

12-17-14

Brad,

I hope you find a few iders you can use inside!

Amanda

JB JOSSEY-BASS™

A Wiley Brand

Published by Jossey-Bass
A Wiley Brand
One Montgomery Street, Suite 1200, San Francisco, CA 94104-4594—
www.josseybass.com

Jossey-Bass books and products are available through most bookstores. To contact Jossey-Bass directly call our Customer Care Department within the U.S. at 800-956-7739, outside the U.S. at 317-572-3986, or fax 317-572-4002.

Wiley publishes in a variety of print and electronic formats and by print-on-demand. Some material included with standard print versions of this book may not be included in e-books or in print-on-demand. If this book refers to media such as a CD or DVD that is not included in the version you purchased, you may download this material at http://booksupport.wiley.com. For more information about Wiley products, visit www.wiley.com.

Library of Congress Cataloging-in-Publication Data

Setili, Amanda, 1959-
   The agility advantage : how to identify and act on opportunities in a fast-changing world / Amanda Setili.—First edition.
      pages cm
   Inclues bibliographical references and index.
   ISBN 978-1-118-83638-5 (hardback); ISBN 978-1-118-96444-6 (pdf);
ISBN 978-1-118-96443-9 (epub)
   1. Strategic planning. 2. Diffusion of innovations. 3. Organizational change. I. Title.
   HD30.28.S396 2014
   658.4'012—dc23

Printed in the United States of America

FIRST EDITION

HB Printing   10 9 8 7 6 5 4 3 2 1

To Rob, Shannon, and Alison

Contents

Preface

In 2011, I founded the Strategic Agility® Think Tank. My goal in establishing this community of corporate peers—CEOs, division presidents, CFOs, CMOs, and leaders in sales, marketing, operations, and strategy—was for them to share ideas and best practices, better navigate their greatest challenges, and become more adept at seeing and capturing new market opportunities.

The community includes leaders of such companies as AT&T, AutoTrader, Best Buy, Bosch, Cbeyond, Cisco, Costco, Cox Communications, Equifax, Fiserv, Georgia-Pacific, Hilton, Intuit, Kraft, J. M. Huber, MeadWestvaco, Time Warner, UPS, and Xerox. The members of this group have learned from one another, and I've learned from them. Along the way, they have strengthened their organizational and personal performance, and I've gained more—and more varied—experience in helping companies navigate change.

My aim in writing this book is to help all organizations—large, established companies with huge investments in the status quo, as well as smaller, younger companies that are relatively light on their feet—become more nimble. In the pages that follow, you'll find examples, tools, and techniques to do just that.

The Impetus for This Book

I wrote this book after more than two decades of working with some of the world's leading companies, including Coca-Cola, Delta Air Lines, The Home Depot, Kimberly-Clark, and

Walmart—companies that are, for the most part, *great* at what they do. Over the years, they had honed their operations, refined their products, and developed brands recognized worldwide. Planes ran on time, product flowed to store shelves, diaper innovations kept this year's babies drier than last year's. Yet the very things that made these companies so good at what they did—the hundreds of thousands of employees, the wealth of technology, and the assets spread across the globe—made it very difficult for them to respond effectively to change.

Change came in many forms for these companies, and from many different directions at once: deregulation, low-cost competitors, disruptive technologies, housing market ups and downs, private-label products, cultural trends—the list goes on and on.

In engagement after engagement, I helped my clients deal with the same basic question: How do we identify opportunities for growth, avoid threats on the horizon, and take advantage of market transformations to bring more value to customers and achieve a lasting advantage over our competitors?

What You Can Gain

If your markets are changing, which they almost always are, what can you do to stay ahead? In a word, you cultivate agility. I define *agility* as the ability to identify new opportunities and capitalize on them quickly. By following the principles, using the tools, and learning from the numerous real-world examples and case studies in this book, you can make your own organization more agile—and have change work to your advantage.

In these pages, I'll let you know how you can anticipate change and be prepared for it when it arrives, armed with the repertoire and resources required to deal effectively with what is ahead. You'll learn how to make sound decisions when data is scarce and the future is uncertain; how to navigate, experiment, and motivate when a sharp turn in strategic direction is required; and how to execute in a flexible way, so that you can adjust your course over time as further change occurs.

A Caveat

The companies I showcase in this book each demonstrate traits important for strategic agility. But they don't have it all figured out; no one does. Technological advances, changes in leadership, financial pressures, regulatory changes, and other events will affect their—and your—future business success.

The processes and systems you put in place to augment agility sometimes fall by the wayside or become outdated as fortunes change. Many companies are agile at one point in time, but later become rigid and insular. Sears Roebuck showed great agility in the 1950s. It later became one of the most calcified companies in the world, and now has a reputation for being out of touch with the market. Dell pioneered many methods for adapting quickly to market changes; specifically, its just-in-time supply chain innovations and systems for customizing product to meet each individual customer's needs were groundbreaking. However, the company has lost its luster of late. IBM, in contrast, was known as an old-line, hierarchical company, yet has become extremely agile in recent years and transformed itself into a completely different organization than it once was.

How to Get the Most out of This Book

I realize that your time is limited, so I've tried to make this book as practical and navigable as possible, with bite-sized pieces that you can pick and choose as your circumstances change. Adapt the tools and frameworks to your own situation. Use the processes, diagnostics, and techniques in meetings and projects. Play with them, twist them around, and modify them. But avoid the temptation to skim over the examples just because you play in a different arena. Tear them apart and critique them—but learn from them and adapt some aspect of them to your own situation. You can learn powerful lessons from industries other than your own, lessons that can confer unique competitive advantages.

Above all, notice and talk about changes you are seeing in your business and marketplace. Ask: What has happened recently that's unexpected, unusual, alarming, or amusing? What opportunities—and pitfalls—do these events reveal?

Writing this book forced me to distill the most agile, adaptive, and successful strategies that I have seen for staying ahead of market changes. It also afforded me the opportunity to revisit and collaborate with past clients and with business leaders I admire. I hope you enjoy reading this book as much as I enjoyed writing it.

Atlanta, Georgia   Amanda Setili
July 2014

THE AGILITY ADVANTAGE

Chapter One

What Is Agility—and Why Is It Valuable?

During the post–World War II boom in home appliances in 1951, General Electric (GE) broke ground on its Appliance Park in Louisville, Kentucky. The complex quickly grew to include six factory buildings the size of shopping malls, and became so immense that it had its own fire department, its own power plant—even its own ZIP code. In 1953, GE purchased a UNIVAC computer to handle payroll, becoming the first business in the world to own a computer (only governments had owned them up until that time).[1] By 1955, Appliance Park employed sixteen thousand workers, and by 1973, twenty-three thousand. During the 1960s, the workers at Appliance Park were turning out sixty thousand appliances each week.

However, something funny happened along the way to the present day.

To cut costs, many American manufacturers moved their factories offshore—to places like Taiwan, Malaysia, the Philippines, Mexico, and China. GE was not immune to this shift; in fact, the company became convinced that to remain competitive, it had no choice but to follow its rivals. This, coupled with ongoing labor disputes, sealed the deal. By 2011, employment at Appliance Park had plunged to just 1,863 people.

However, the cost equation that once made offshoring appear so attractive for U.S. manufacturers has recently been turned upside down. For many, the expected cost savings of offshoring did not materialize. Sure, the overseas factory is lower cost when things are humming along in steady state. But it doesn't take many "unexpected" costs—such as expediting rush orders, flying managers and engineers back and forth to fix problems, or dealing with the repercussions of quality or safety problems—to erase the benefit. Further, contracting with overseas manufacturers requires locking in the design and the assembly process—spelling everything out. Making changes is a big deal when you are managing an outside entity, and a fourteen-hour flight is required just to go observe the process and the people running it.

Further, the cost advantages that led domestic companies to move offshore have in large part receded. Chinese wages, in dollars, rose by a factor of five between 2000 and 2012. Over the same period, oil prices grew threefold, which increased freight costs. Natural gas prices in the United States are now four times lower than in Asia, providing U.S. factories with an energy cost advantage. Relations between U.S. employers and unions have eased, and due to advances in automation, labor is a far smaller proportion of overall product cost than in times past. From a cost perspective, offshoring is not as attractive as it once was; as a result, a growing number of American companies are bringing their manufacturing operations back to the United States. According to Jeffrey Immelt, CEO of GE, offshoring is becoming "outdated as a business model for GE Appliances."[2]

Immelt definitely put his money where his mouth is, investing $800 million in the revitalization of GE's Louisville appliance manufacturing plants. During the course of 2012, GE opened new assembly lines at Appliance Park to manufacture high-end refrigerators and low-energy water heaters. The company added additional assembly lines in 2013 to produce front-loading washing machines and dryers, along with stainless-steel dishwashers.

But making these changes wasn't easy. During the twenty-year period when Chinese and Mexican contract manufacturers, not Kentuckians, were building most of GE's appliances, GE lost expertise in how to build its own products. However, this problem became an opportunity for the company's design and manufacturing engineers and line workers to start with a clean sheet of paper. For example, GE discovered through careful redesign that it could beat the price of the Chinese version of its GeoSpring energy-efficient water heater by 20 percent—delivering its product at a retail price of $1,299 versus $1,599 for the Chinese unit.

This unexpected advantage came about in large part because GE's assembly workers collaborated directly with its designers, engineers, marketers, and others, working in an open, collegial, and self-critical way. More important than the substantial cost reduction, however, is the shorter product development cycle that collocating manufacturing with other functions enables. The ever-quickening pace of product innovation across multiple industries, along with the incorporation of ever-smarter electronics into formerly mature products like home appliances, has significantly shrunk GE's product life cycle. Just a few years ago, an appliance design stayed competitive for seven years; GE's managers now expect a model to last no more than two or three. The factory has become a laboratory for innovation, able to evolve to meet shifting customer demand and to adapt to changing competitive environments.

Delivery times also declined dramatically thanks to the shift back to U.S. manufacturing. Whereas transit time from the Chinese factory to U.S. retailers was five weeks, GE can now move appliances from the Appliance Park factory to Lowe's and Home Depot warehouses in thirty minutes. The company can react to changes in customer demand in days rather than weeks, scaling production up and down in response to increased or declining need. This responsiveness can make a huge difference as competitors roll out new models more frequently. Imagine the savings in inventory costs and in avoiding deep discounting to unload obsolete inventory.

The net result? GE hired seventeen hundred additional U.S. hourly employees in 2012, along with five hundred new engineers and designers from 2009 through the end of 2012. And at the beginning of 2013, the company derived 55 percent of its $5 billion in annual appliance revenue from U.S.-built products. This number is expected to grow to 75 percent by the end of 2014. That's a remarkably fast shift for a huge company like GE. But it goes to show that even the largest businesses can move with great agility if they apply the right approach.

What Is Agility?

In my work with organizations in every industry, I have discovered that the most consistently successful companies—with success defined in terms of growth and profitability—are the most agile. Like GE, these organizations are able to see and respond to changes in the marketplace more capably and quickly than their competitors.

In years past, companies could pick a strategy and stick with it. Perseverance was rewarded. Once they established competitive advantage—whether through lower costs, higher quality, or a superior customer relationship—they could often maintain it for years, even decades. Nowadays, however, change comes faster, and companies can surge ahead of or fall behind competitors in mere months.

As I mentioned in the Preface, *agility* is the ability to see and capitalize on new opportunities *quickly*. It has three components:

- **Market** agility
- **Decision** agility
- **Execution** agility

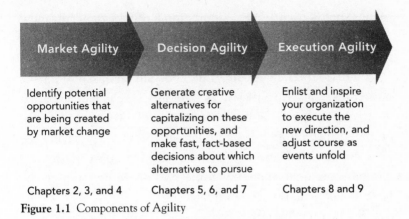

Figure 1.1 Components of Agility

Each of these components is addressed in the chapters of this book, as shown in Figure 1.1.

Each company has unique challenges that threaten its ability to be agile. Some excel at gaining market insights and identifying opportunities, but get bogged down in the decision-making stage and let opportunities pass them by. Others falter in the execution stage. Some execute superbly, but miss market signals—and head fast in the wrong direction as a result. This book will help you strengthen your capabilities across all three areas, so that you can move faster than the market.

BlackBerry (formerly RIM) had a "blinding confidence"[3] in its core product, believing that its large installed base, proprietary network, and superior security features would enable it to maintain market dominance. But the company was too slow to improve, and saw its share of the smartphone market drop from over 40 percent in 2008 to only 5 percent in 2013. BlackBerry's market capitalization is now only about one-twentieth of its peak.

In a similar vein, Microsoft once dominated the technology industry. Since 2000, however, the company has struggled in almost every arena it has entered, including e-books, music players, search, and social networking. Newer players such as Google and Facebook have raced by Microsoft and radically changed the way we live. Although Microsoft recognized growth opportunities, it was unable to take the right action quickly enough. As a result, Microsoft's market capitalization has increased only about 10 percent in the twelve years ending in June 2014, while Apple's market capitalization increased by more than ninety times.

In 2013, Intel chairman Andrew Bryant admitted to having missed the tablet market. "The future is simple; computing devices are going to be smaller," Bryant said. "We were in denial of tablets, [which] put us in a hole, and [now] we're paying the price for that."[4] Because Intel focused on its historically very profitable personal computer business, it missed investing in the large and obvious trend toward tablets.

Blockbuster, Borders, Sears/Kmart, and Hewlett-Packard have similarly fallen from their prominent positions and have not recovered, at least to date.

What was the cause of these companies' troubles? Each had smart people and resources to spare, but they ignored the signs that change was needed. In some cases, they failed to see opportunities to capitalize on change; in others, they recognized an opportunity but failed to act in a timely and effective way. I have observed five primary obstacles to achieving agility:

- Companies lose touch with customers, and leaders lose touch with their own employees. As a result, they receive poor, late, biased, or no information at all about emerging customer needs, changes in competitor capabilities, or the possibilities new technologies are creating. When a new opportunity does arise, they often fail to see and act on it.
- Companies employ financial incentives that motivate short-term thinking and doing "more of the same." To compound this, many leaders do not know how to deal with unpredictability in a systematic way. They therefore hesitate to take action without irrefutable data supporting the new direction.
- Leaders become wrapped up in daily challenges and business as usual, which keeps them from investing time in imagining what the future might hold or how they might take advantage

of coming changes. They fail to effectively bridge corporate silos and encourage real debate regarding their company's future direction.

- Organizational structure gets in the way. I recently met with an executive at a leading supplier of financial services technologies. I knew that the company had identified a major new product opportunity more than five years ago, so I asked him how they were moving ahead. "We haven't made much progress," he explained. "The capabilities we need to pursue this are spread across three or four different business units. Each would get credit for only a small portion of the revenue, so they have little incentive to go after the opportunity."

- Even if companies see opportunities and make a timely decision to pursue them, leaders often fail to communicate the compelling, inspiring vision required to harness their employees' full energy, creativity, and agility.

Business Models Are Evolving Fast—with New Winners and New Losers

Every industry undergoes change. The players who devise a different and better way of capitalizing on the transformations they witness are the ones that emerge as winners.

Few arenas have experienced more change in the last decade than the music industry. It was the first mass-media industry to be hammered by the digital revolution, and it shrank from $38 billion in annual revenues a little more than a decade ago to somewhat less than half that figure—$16.5 billion—in 2012.[5] This contraction provides a dramatic example of how revenue sources can quickly shift as new businesses and business models are introduced into the market.

New ways to sell music appear every year, and old ones wither. Years ago, performers made their money selling albums, and went on tour mainly to promote those albums. Now the economics have flipped: concerts comprise more than half of industry revenues,[6] and bands release albums mainly as marketing pieces to attract fans to fill concert halls. Performers now have new sources of revenue, including merchandise sales, YouTube ads, licensing to television and film productions, iTunes downloads, and royalties from streaming music services such as Spotify, Rhapsody, and Muve Music and from Internet radio stations including Pandora, Slacker, and iHeartRadio.[7] Music industry revenue hasn't just shrunk; it's coming from completely new sources.

The enormously complex and quickly evolving newspaper industry is another example of a business model that's shifted substantially over time. Newspapers used to rely on advertising and subscription sales, but as these revenue sources have dried up—with print ad revenue dropping from $44.9 billion in 2003 to $18.9 billion in 2012[8]—publishers have had to find new sources. Some are garnering income from conferences, which take in sponsorship revenue and attendance fees, or by helping small businesses develop and manage their Web and mobile presence and their daily deals.

Amazon CEO Jeff Bezos, who purchased the *Washington Post* in 2013, believes that the newspaper's readers would be willing to pay for a bundled information product that provides them with real value. Says Bezos, "There are so many knobs that can be turned and things we can experiment with, that I'm confident there's something we can find that readers will love and will be engaged with—and that we can charge for."[9] Of course, exactly *what* that something would be is the $250 million question (the amount Bezos paid for the *Post* and a few related assets).[10] But now that the *Post* has become a distant relation of Amazon, the potential synergies and partnerships between the two organizations are virtually unlimited and may very well fill in the blanks.

If you are going to stay in business these days, you need to continuously evolve, change, and stay a step or two ahead of your competitors.

What Kind of Companies Need to Be Agile?

In today's turbulent market environment, historical drivers of success, such as operational excellence, brand, and financial resources, no longer assure survival. Future competitive advantage will require the ability to rapidly and continuously adapt to market change.

The kinds of companies that especially need to be agile are those in "fast-moving" industries: technology, e-commerce, mobile handsets, and software, certainly. But what about quick-serve restaurants? Yes! What about pulp and paper, or specialty chemicals? Yes! What about basic materials and oil? Yes!

The short answer is that companies in *every* industry need to become more agile.

Throughout this book, we'll look at examples from technology-based firms, such as Amazon, Apple, Facebook, Google, and Samsung. However, agility is not limited just to high tech. We'll also examine other industries, such as travel (Airbnb, Delta Air Lines, Hilton), food service (Arby's, Starbucks), automotive (Ford, Tata, Tesla), consumer products and services (AT&T, Haier, Kimberly-Clark, UPS), and industrial (AGCO, EnPro Industries, GE).

What We See in Agile Organizations

When an organization is agile, employees are alert. They anticipate what might happen next. They see opportunities and decide quickly and capably which to pursue. They move fast when action is needed—and after they take action, they monitor the situation assiduously to ensure that the intended results come to pass, and to take additional action when necessary. It's a pleasure to lead and work in these organizations. People care. They have energy. They jump on new ideas and are eager to reach across functional lines—or to partners outside the organization—to innovate. They are decisive.

In contrast, organizations that are not agile are complacent and insular. These organizations' leaders are often out of touch with customers and the front line. They repeatedly defer or ignore decisions on important issues. When these companies do take action, it often peters out or unravels due to lack of clarity and commitment. Employees at all levels have "checked out" of the competitive game.

Agile companies possess the following five characteristics:

- **Sharpened senses.** Employees maintain a continuous and keen awareness of emerging customer needs, new technology trends, likely competitor moves, changes in supplier markets, and the like. Like a mill horse with its nose to the grindstone, employees can be blinded to what's around them by the busyness and monotony of daily operations. Because changes like emerging customer interest in a certain product feature or discontent with another happen gradually, they go unnoticed. Agile organizations, however, are highly sensitive to market changes. They grant employees leeway to do something about the changes they see; as a result, employees notice more changes earlier, and react more immediately and effectively.

- **Clarity and objectivity.** Agile companies are objective about their own shortcomings and about where they excel. They are able to make sense of many market changes simultaneously and can zero in on those that are important, while resisting the "sensory overload" that can lead to paralysis. They are able to rationally and proactively deal with the uncertainties and risks inherent in any new initiative or strategic direction. They are willing to shed portions of the business that do not fit with their new direction, rather than becoming emotionally attached to "the way we've always done things." Their clear and objective understanding of the current situation allows them to be more adept at projecting what might happen next.

- **Ingenuity, resourcefulness, and openness to change.** When a company faces a difficult strategic situation, its executives may see few strategic options and feel boxed into a corner. But an agile organization can identify new strategic alternatives. Much as the human brain goes into overdrive when a threat is near, an agile organization responds positively to change, firing the synapses between functions, spurring creativity, and identifying nonobvious and groundbreaking strategic options.

- **Fast, rational decision making.** Companies often get bogged down in indecision for months when assessing a potential change in strategy; they're busy dealing with stakeholder objections and fretting over risks. Although objections are usually legitimate, they're also generally surmountable. Agile companies consider all the facts, risks, and stakeholder concerns and then make a quick decision about which direction to take.

- **Committed yet flexible action.** Agile companies implement aggressively while anticipating change and building in flexibility to make course corrections. They are very much like a skier heading down a black diamond slope—committed to the path, maximally alert, and ready to respond to the unexpected to navigate through the rough territory. Because the skier cannot see far ahead, he anticipates and prepares for what he might encounter. He keeps his hips and knees loose and flexible. He uses the terrain to his advantage, working with the mountain, rather than against it. He's fluid, almost musical, in his agility. He lets his adrenaline work for him—just as agile companies do.

Changes in Technology, Culture, and the Economy Are Driving the Need for Greater Agility

There are a variety of different factors driving the faster pace of change and the need for greater agility. Each one has a greater or lesser impact, depending on an organization's specific situation. The six that follow are, in my experience, the most important.

Globalization

Cultures and economies have become interconnected across the globe in ways we would not have thought possible a decade or two ago. The balance of economic power is shifting to China, India, Brazil, and other emerging economies—and the vast majority of consumers in these fast-changing markets want very low priced products that consumers in the developed world might consider "inferior." Yet some companies have learned to serve these needs quite profitably. For example, Vodafone's M-PESA mobile-money service is targeted at people without access to conventional banking and enables money transfers, loans, and salary disbursements via text messaging technology. Two-thirds of the adults in Kenya, where the service has been highly successful, now use the system, and about 25 percent of the country's gross national product flows through it. Companies that adapt effectively to unfamiliar markets while maintaining the scale advantages of being a global operator will be extremely successful.

Microcultures

Electronic media have enabled microcultures—highly specific interest groups that span geographies—to proliferate, as like-minded people find one another and communicate across boundaries and social strata. Thus I may have more in common with someone in a tiny country halfway around the world—a person who shares with me a similar set of values and interests—than I do with my next-door neighbor. These microcultures, which are effectively self-segmenting customer groups, can be very profitable markets for companies that can cater to them cost-effectively. Examples of microcultures include endurance obstacle course racers, golden retriever lovers (served by in-home boarding companies like Just Goldens and Only Goldens), frequent travelers (who trade ideas on FlyerTalk), antique boat owners (and the restorers and parts suppliers that serve them), and costuming aficionados.

Collaboration

Customers increasingly contribute to or even perform functions formerly deemed "internal"—such as marketing, product development, technical support, and sales. At the same time, electronic media have opened doors for employees to collaborate and communicate far more easily and frequently across corporate functions, with partners, and directly with customers. Customers are more willing than ever to share resources—cars, homes, and the like—through "collaborative consumption." Fostering and providing a platform for this collaboration can be an effective vehicle for reducing costs, gaining visibility into customer needs, and speeding up the innovation cycle.

Technology Changes

New technologies are created daily, product life cycles are shortening, and intellectual property is increasingly difficult to protect. Many products serve functions and fill needs that didn't even exist a few years ago. (Did you really *need* a smart phone or a tablet computer a few years ago?) New developments cross nanotechnology, biotechnology, neuroscience, genomics, materials, wireless-connected sensors, data analytics, and information technology. It frequently astonishes me when I realize that something which seems as though it has been part of my life for a long, long time was introduced only three or four years ago. Even "low-tech" companies must understand and exploit these new technologies to avoid falling behind.

Transparency and Customer Power

Word travels fast nowadays. Customer reactions to products, communications, and corporate actions are immediate and unfiltered. A company's impact on the environment, health, and social welfare is far more visible and more closely scrutinized than ever before. It's gotten much trickier to manage brand and public opinion over time, yet we also reap the benefit of gaining greater visibility into what customers are thinking. We can test products, price points, and communication strategy on the Web, and get feedback in minutes as to which option is the most effective.

Commoditization

Amid all these trends that affect our businesses, there is one that is ever present and more menacing than ever before. In industry after industry, the endless onslaught of commoditization takes its toll, as it has been doing for hundreds of years.

Some companies have successfully maintained differentiation —or at least brand preference—but it is becoming increasingly difficult to do so. Technology has made comparison-shopping effortless for consumers, and bidding and auction processes have become more common in business transactions. As the products and services that various competitors offer become increasingly similar, prices are driven down.

A Sears Craftsman brand electric circular saw cost $100 in 1950—the equivalent of $970 in today's dollars.[11] Today, a Craftsman circular saw can be purchased on the Sears website for $29.74, *thirty-two times less* in real dollars than sixty-five years ago. The Amazon website lists circular saws from Black and Decker, DeWalt, Hitachi, Makita, Porter-Cable, Ridgid, Robert Bosch, Rockwell, Ryobi, Skil, and others. Although it is true that some of these saws retail for far more than $30 (depending on features), there's no doubt that commoditization has driven prices down in this highly competitive market.

Replication of competitors' services and products has become more commonplace, as companies can easily outsource almost any element of their value chain—from R&D to manufacturing to sales and marketing.

At the same time, intellectual property has become harder to protect as the speed and fluidity of information sharing and global trade have increased. Patents ensure only that you will keep your attorneys busy. Just look at the multiyear patent dispute between

Apple and Samsung; together, the two companies have invested over a billion dollars in the legal battle, with no apparent effect on their relative standing in the marketplace.[12]

Increase Agility Where It Makes the Most Difference

Attempting to achieve agility across all aspects of your business—all functions, geographies, and product lines—can often produce conflicting priorities, thereby bringing any forward motion to a grinding halt. It's therefore important to focus your agility-enhancing efforts on those parts of your business where agility can have the greatest impact on your overall success. For example, Samsung chooses to manufacture most offerings internally; the company cites this capability as a major strength that enables it to quickly and effectively bring new products to market. However, Samsung *does* rely on outsourcing for peripheral products, such as components and handset cases, for which adaptability is less important. This is why it's worthwhile to *explicitly identify* the areas of your business where agility is most important, and where it is less so.

Recently, our fourteen-year-old clothes dryer stopped working, and we needed a new one. My husband had been doing online research on brands, features, and prices. I was driving home when I passed by BrandsMart, a store I had heard good things about. I knew they carried appliances, so I pulled into the parking lot. The salesperson was very knowledgeable and quite good at diagnosing my needs to make a specific product recommendation. But I ended up carrying out much of my decision-making process online. I wanted to know about other customers' experience with each model I was considering, compare prices at other stores, and see if there were any special offers available. Ultimately, we bought our new dryer at BrandsMart—but not before we had done our research online.

Just like any company, BrandsMart has limited resources and busy managers. They don't have time to worry about everything at once. The company must focus its agility efforts on those areas that will make the most difference to its overall success. So how does a company like this decide which elements of its business require the most agility and which can be left relatively stable? Where does it need to be most attentive to new trends and customer needs and most flexible to make changes quickly? Figure 1.2 shows how an appliance and electronics retailer like BrandsMart could answer two key questions to determine where it should focus its efforts:

- To what extent, and how quickly, is the business environment changing? (the x-axis)
- To what extent does this part of your business affect the customer's decision to buy from you? (the y-axis)

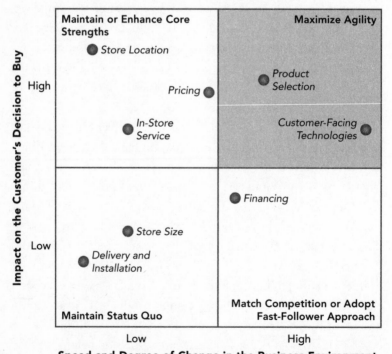

Figure 1.2 The Setili Agility Framework (Appliance and Electronics Retailer Example)

BrandsMart—or any company, for that matter—should focus its attention on increasing agility in those elements of its business for which the answer is "high" to both of these questions. That is, they should focus on those business elements where the business environment is changing fast *and* there is a great impact on the customer's decision to buy (the top right quadrant).

A major factor affecting a customer's decision about where to buy is store location—an element you see in the figure's top left corner. Just as I impulsively swung into the BrandsMart parking lot, a customer is unlikely to drive by a nearby store on his or her way to one farther from home—unless the more distant store is substantially superior in some way, offering significantly better product selection, service, or prices, for example. This is why store location is shown as "high" on the y-axis, which measures impact on the customer's decision to buy.

However, the *business environment* with respect to store location—shown on the graph's x-axis—changes rather slowly. Neighborhoods that are strong markets for appliances and electronics, and intersections that are convenient to major commuting routes, are likely to stay strong for years—even decades. Further, a new store represents a substantial investment; once built, it's difficult for the retailer to relocate. Therefore, location is a relatively stable element of business.

Product selection greatly impacts a customer's decision to buy, and is subject to much change in the business environment. New features are introduced frequently, and consumer lifestyles and buying preferences are constantly evolving. If the store has the wrong products in stock relative to consumer tastes, margin-damaging markdowns are inevitable. The company must be able to read the market and offer the products that people want to buy each year. Therefore, product selection appears in the shaded top right box of the figure: it has a high impact on customers' decision to buy, and the business environment is changing quickly. This is the area where the retailer needs to focus its agility.

Customer-facing technologies, such as the company's website, mobile apps, and point-of-sale payment options, have relatively less influence on the customer's decision to buy. However, these technologies are transforming very quickly, which puts this component in the top right box of our chart—an area in which the retailer would be smart to maximize agility. New mobile-shopping applications, recommendation engines, and consumer payment technologies are introduced into the market almost continuously. And customers *do* buy more—and more often—from retailers that provide technologies that allow customers to easily discover, research, pay for, use, and even return products.

Customer-facing technologies garner benefits beyond getting customers to buy more. Retail giant Nordstrom is known for its legendary customer service—something they're clearly maintaining as technology evolves. Their newest stores have more mobile devices for accepting payment than fixed ones. When a sales associate can process payments in the middle of the store, far from the register, she can continue to engage a customer about that product—and others—generating more sales. If she sees that the customer is close to an upgrade in the Nordstrom loyalty program, she can suggest buying a little more so that he qualifies. This system benefits customers by eliminating the need to stand in boring, time-consuming lines—and it benefits Nordstrom in the form of increased sales and improved customer satisfaction. Indeed, same-store sales have risen far more for Nordstrom than for its peers, about 7.5 percent per year in the 2010–2013 time frame.[13]

Where Is Agility Most Important in Your Business?

To apply this framework to your situation, use Table 1.1 to list the elements of your business that affect the customer's decision to buy. In a business-to-business market, these may include things like product design, quality-management systems, technical support, sales, quotations, installation-and-repair services, inventory control systems, and order-processing systems. List not only the

Table 1.1 Determining Where Agility Is Most Important in Your Business

Elements of your value-delivery system	Degree of impact on the customer's decision to buy (the y-axis—rate on 1–10 scale)	Degree of change in the business environment (the x-axis—rate on 1–10 scale)
1.		
2.		
3.		
4.		
5.		
6.		

elements of the way you *currently* do business but also things you are considering *adding* to enhance your offering.

Next, assess each one's degree of impact on the customer's decision to buy (the y-axis) and the degree of change in the business environment (the x-axis). The business elements that rank high on both—landing in the top right box—are the ones for which you need to be most agile. Focus here on improving your ability to sense changes in the market, to make fast decisions about which changes to pursue, and to act on these decisions quickly and capably.

Every company will draw different conclusions about where agility is most important. McDonald's must be agile in its menu and marketing communication, but may be relatively stable in terms of franchisee and supplier relations.

Whether you use the technique described here or some other process, it's crucial to determine where agility is most critical in your business—and then to concentrate your efforts there. This will consistently give you the greatest return on your investment of both human and financial capital.

In the chapters that follow, we'll dive deeply into each of the three components of agility, deriving tactics and strategies that any company in any industry can apply to stay ahead of its competition and benefit from market change.

Chapter Two

See Through Your Customers' Eyes

How to See What Your Competitor Can't

From the time Amazon was a tiny company, founder and CEO Jeff Bezos has regularly scanned customer emails, sometimes even ignoring the discussion at his own meetings as he does so. He immediately forwards both complaints and ideas for innovations and improvements to the people in his organization who can act on them, and expects them to do so promptly.

Most CEOs rely on lower-level employees to conduct such time-consuming customer intelligence. CEOs who *do* read customer emails might even feel guilty for not spending their time on more important company matters, like setting budgets, communicating with Wall Street, or discussing financial results with their team. "Other companies have more of a *conqueror* mentality," Bezos says. "We think of ourselves as explorers." Staying in tune with what customers are thinking and how they are responding to Amazon service, features, and products is a key part of this exploration.

Bezos asserts that *customer focus* distinguishes Amazon from other companies, which tend to concentrate on competing brands when setting strategy. "When they're in the shower in the morning, they're thinking about how they're going to get ahead of one of their top competitors," Bezos says. "Here in the shower, we're thinking about how we are going to invent something on behalf of a customer."[1]

It's impossible to know exactly why Bezos has given Amazon's customers such an important role in the company. However, much seems due to his unique mixture of groundedness (Bezos spent many summers growing up doing chores at his grandparents' Texas cattle ranch), quantitative genius (he graduated from Princeton with a BS degree in electrical engineering and computer science), and big thinking (he wanted to be an astronaut and founded aerospace company Blue Origin in 2000 with the goal of helping "anybody to go into space").

Each year, Amazon turns dozens of unsolicited customer ideas into feature improvements. The site makes buying incredibly easy; it always seems to know what a given customer wants, and has it available at prices that few stores—whether on- or offline—can beat. And because the online reviews are so incredibly helpful, customers seldom suffer from buyer's remorse when they shop at Amazon. It's no surprise to me that Amazon has led the University of Michigan customer satisfaction index for online retailers for years, and has repeatedly placed in the top ten among all companies.

Bezos expects thousands of Amazon managers—including himself—to attend two days of call-center training each year. This training enhances the Amazon mindset around listening to, empathizing with, and understanding the customer. This mindset and constant exploration of customer needs have allowed Amazon to make move after move that has sent its stock soaring 47 percent per year for the last five years. And with the *Washington Post* purchase, observers are wondering—and, in many cases, *hoping*—that some of the same financial magic will rub off on this old-line analog industry that is struggling to find its way in today's digital world.

What can your company do to adopt a customer mindset, to see through the customer's eyes, and to identify more opportunities that enhance customer value? How can you build market awareness into your everyday activities by mixing with customers, using competitor products, or using your own product as a customer would?

We will explore these questions as we discover what companies in a variety of industries are doing to see through their customers' eyes.

Amazon Doesn't Care (Much) About Wall Street

While Amazon's revenue growth is excellent—the company brought in more than $74 billion in 2013, an increase of 22 percent from the previous year—investors are often concerned about the company's long-term prospects because profitability is not so great. (Amazon booked a net loss of $39 million for 2012 and a small profit in 2013.) This is due to Bezos's long-term view; he doesn't worry much about short-term earnings, and he has a "mild disdain" for what Wall Street thinks—an admirable perspective.

Back in 1999, when Amazon was still really small and was selling only books, I attended a breakout session on e-commerce at a Harvard Business School reunion. Another alumna, Joy Covey, was CFO and head of strategy for Amazon at the time. Someone in the audience asked when Amazon was going to become profitable, implying that it had been in business long enough and that it was high time the company showed some profits. I'll never forget Joy's answer.

She said, "It costs us $4 to acquire each additional customer—when would *you* stop?" Joy's answer was very thought provoking, and it shed light on Bezos's long-term strategy, which seems to be: "First acquire lots of customers, then sell them everything they could possibly want."

Experience What Customers Do, Firsthand

For many years now, countless engineers, product designers, and executives who work for Apple Inc.'s competitors have wondered how the company always seems to be a step ahead of everyone else in the marketplace.

Apple is obviously doing something right. The average selling price of its smartphones was twice as high (at over $635 in third-quarter 2013) as its competitors on the Google Android and Microsoft Windows platforms (whose average smartphone selling price is about $300).[2] Apple, however, does not take Bezos's approach of asking customers what features *they* want in the next product. "We do no market research," said Steve Jobs in a 2008 interview with *Fortune*. "We figure out what we want. And I think we're pretty good at having the right discipline to think through whether a lot of other people are going to want it, too. That's what we get paid to do."[3]

Have you ever encountered a problem when using a product and thought to yourself, "Have the people who designed this product ever even *used it themselves*? How could they not have noticed this?" It's astonishing how frequently we encounter decision makers who have little to no experience using their own company's products. Less common, but perhaps even more mystifying, are companies that have an unwritten rule *discouraging* employees from using its competitors' products.

Everyday use of your own *and your competitors'* products and services can open your eyes about where your offerings are lacking, and how and where you can create more value. It's important, though, to keep an open mind when you're considering a competitor's product. It's extremely easy to fall into the trap of thinking that because it's your competitor's, it's no good. Instead, take a moment to recognize that natural bias, then remove it from your mind. Imagine that you are a typical consumer, and feel what it's like to fall in love with your competitor's product—or at least to be impartial. Although difficult, it's essential for you to do this if you wish to gain insights on where you can improve and how you can differentiate your products from your competitors'.

When you are using your own product or that of a competitor, ask yourself the questions listed in Table 2.1.

When Delta Air Lines wanted to improve its customer experience, the company's top management team was asked to "fly like a customer." This meant going through the process of using the Delta website to find flights and buy tickets online, wait through long security lines at the airport, and sit in cramped coach seats—everything Delta's typical customers experienced. Normally, a top airline executive's flying experience—complete with free tickets reserved and picked up by an assistant, zipping

Table 2.1 Questions to Ask When Using Your Own Product or a Competitor's

To Discover . . .	Ask Yourself . . .
Alternative solutions	• What problem was I trying to solve when I chose to use this product or service? • In what other ways could I solve that problem?
Enhancement opportunities	• What's really frustrating to me when I use this product? • What new problems does using the product create? • What could be eliminated or reduced? • What's missing? • How could the experience be faster or more enjoyable? • What undesirable variability occurs in the product or in how it's delivered? What problems come as a result? • What might I like to customize?
Adjacencies	• What other versions of this product would be nice to have? • What other products or services might I want when I am using this product? • What do I do right before and after using the product? (Is there a role for my company to play in these parts of the process?)
Ways to improve awareness and availability	• When might I want to use the product? Is it convenient to obtain it in each of these situations? • If I wanted to tell a colleague or friend about this product, how would I do so? What if I wanted to give a positive review or to talk about it online?

through security lines, and sitting in first class—is nothing like a typical customer's. So you can imagine the insights they gained.

As a result of experiencing these pain points firsthand, Delta's leaders creatively innovated enhancements in check-in procedures, gate assistance, onboard food and beverage service, seat comfort, overhead bin design, safety announcements, and more.

For perhaps the ultimate example of a company that gets close to its customers, we look at workers at the headquarters of Mars, Inc.'s pet food division—which produces the Whiskas and Pedigree brands—who are allowed to bring their dogs to work. About half of the 475 employees do just that, several days a week. Says Tiffany Bierer, the division's head of health and nutritional sciences, "I've tasted everything we make." Yes—that means everything from canned cat food with "gravy" to doggie biscuits (Bierer's personal favorite) and all the rest. Mars also keeps cats on hand so that employees can better understand their personalities, likes, and dislikes.

In addition to gaining experience as a user of your own products, be sure to employ people who are—or, at least, who *think like*—your users. If you sell to young people, listen to your interns, and place them in parts of your business that need a shot of innovation or a fresh view on the young customers' experience. If you sell to mechanics, employ mechanics. If you sell to doctors and nurses, be sure to include a few of those on your staff.

Put Customers to Work

Salesforce.com involves customers in product innovation and service. Threadless, an online community and e-commerce website, enlists customers as designers. Makers of everything from toilets to laptops get customers to post homemade product demos on YouTube. Thousands of companies rely on user-generated content for technical support and troubleshooting—and the continued growth of social media essentially guarantees that this trend will continue to expand in reach for the foreseeable future.

One reason why smart companies like Salesforce.com and Threadless are making it easy for customers to pitch in on product development, technical support, sales, and marketing is that customers can often perform these roles in a lower-cost, higher-quality way than can employees. However, an even more important reason is that doing so *expands the interface* between the companies and their customers. When you enlist your customers to get involved, you rub shoulders with them more often. As a result, you gain new ideas and get excited about those ideas—you become personally invested in seeing them through. You hear about customer frustrations more frequently—and those frustrations seem real and pressing.

As employees observe and interact with customers who help in these ways, they often encounter energizing surprises. Customers solve product problems in unexpected ways and develop new uses for products—and ideas for enhancing and improving them that company insiders never imagined.

You might assume that customer research is an equally effective way to gain these insights. However, the trouble with research is that you often find only what you are specifically looking for. In reality, you don't know what you don't know—and true insights are often obscured as a result. Actually *putting customers to work* yields insights you are not seeking, that you did not expect—and that you can capitalize on to spur growth and improve company performance.

Why Conventional Market Research Often Misses New Trends

Conventional market research is often not a good way to see market change or to identify new opportunities. Here's why it often misses new trends:

- **Traditional market research often focuses on your biggest, most established customers.** Although you do need to understand these important customers, tomorrow's business may come from individuals or companies that are not buying much—or anything—from you today. Conventional market research usually overlooks these customers.

- **The people who participate in surveys, focus groups, and interviews—especially in business-to-business markets—often are *not* the people you need to be listening to.** Instead, the people you want to have answer surveys, those with the greatest insights on what's likely to come next, typically have little time or patience for such things—because they are busy running businesses.

- **You see only what you are looking for.** Because companies tend to ask questions based on their current business, market research often misses the new ideas. So even though you do usually get the answer to the question you asked, you may be left wondering, Did I ask the right question in the first place?

- **Customers don't know, or at least often can't articulate, what they would like next.** Customers are pretty good at saying yes or no *once they experience a product*. They are largely incapable, however, of *predicting* their need for a product or feature they have not yet tried. Like companies, they just don't know what they don't know.

- **Emotions drive customer decisions.** The *Economist* reports that "over 85% of consumer buying behavior is driven by the non-conscious," adding, "Recent published findings in neuroscience indicate it is emotion, not reason, that drives our purchasing decisions."* This holds true for business-to-business buying decisions as well. We try, as professionals, to make buying decisions based on objective criteria; but in the end, emotions usually drive our purchases. The desire for our colleagues' admiration may drive us toward the splashy, innovative business purchase, while fear may drive us toward the "safest" choice. Just look at the maxim, "No one ever got fired for buying IBM." A researcher could potentially ask me, "Would you prefer to buy from company X and take a risk of getting fired, or from IBM and incur no such risk?" but it would be difficult for her to incite the subtle and unconscious emotions that might actually guide my buying decision. Market research is not good at simulating the exact circumstances and emotions that surround and influence a customer's buying decision.

*"Retail Therapy," *Economist,* December 17, 2011, http://www .economist.com/node/21541706.

Customers *are* willing to pitch in—*if* you make it easy for them to get involved. To draw customers into your business, think about the answers to these questions:

- **What role could customers play in doing your business's work?**
  o Could they help *drive innovation* by suggesting or testing new materials, designs, or services? Dell and others rely heavily on user suggestions to guide their innovation priorities and to beta-test new features.
  o Could they play a role in *producing* your product or *performing* your service? Consider how IKEA enlists customers to select, pull from the warehouse, transport, and then assemble their own furniture.
  o What role could customers play in *marketing*—qualifying and referring customers, spreading the word about your product, or helping other customers choose the best model for their needs? Home Depot provides an online community in which DIYers can share design, renovation, and lawn-and-garden ideas. Armed with this information

and inspired by others who have solved a similar problem, customers gain confidence to take on more, larger—and therefore, more expensive—DIY projects.

o   How can they help *other users use* and maintain your product? For example, Google, Microsoft, and Livescribe customers provide technical support to others through forums, and Salesforce.com customers regularly create customized applications and enhancements that other companies can adopt.

o   How would customers like to sell, give, or dispose of your product when they have *finished using it*? Best Buy makes it very easy to trade in a used phone. Customers simply find the model they want to trade in on the company website; if they like the price Best Buy offers, they can ship the phone to the company and receive a gift card in exchange. A 16GB iPhone 4, for example, is worth $75 using this system. Even if the trade-in value is small, it does help customers feel that their used equipment is going "to a good home," or at least being recycled responsibly. Perhaps more important, they can trust Best Buy to wipe their personal data from the phone before redeploying it.

- **What are your objectives in getting customers involved in each of these activities?** Will it reduce cost, increase market share, or improve your brand image? For example, Coca-Cola engages customers in designing new beverage can graphics as a way to enhance brand awareness and affinity; IKEA asks customers to assemble their own furniture not just to reduce cost but to increase the customers' affinity for the product.

- **What might the customers' objectives be for getting involved?** What are the benefits for customers? Some might be seeking to enhance their public profile or reputation (and there's nothing wrong with that). But many get involved out of the simple desire to collaborate and interact with like-minded people who use and love the same product.

- **What structure or processes should you put in place to make it easy for the customer to get involved?** Find out where, how, when, and with whom customers wish to interact, then build the systems or programs to enable them to do so. These could take the form of a physical workshop, a conference or meeting, an online tool or community, or a one-on-one outreach to business-to-business customers.

Table 2.2 provides a template for thinking about these questions, along with some examples.

In many cases, participation seems to be its own reward for customers who perform such work. For example, the benefits Salesforce.com provides to its one hundred or so highest-contributing "MVPs" seem mainly to be opportunities to contribute even more in the way of advocacy and service to other customers and to the company. The Salesforce.com website lists the following rewards for being an MVP:

- Highlighted achievements on our blog and at Salesforce Events
- An accolade for their resume and elevated status in the community
- Invitations to speaking opportunities at Dreamforce and other events
- Access to Salesforce Executives at exclusive MVP networking events
- Special briefings with members of our product and marketing teams
- MVP networking events with Salesforce executives
- A Rickshaw laptop bag which is a unique gift all our MVPs receive

It's very interesting—and a perfect example of the psychology that companies like Salesforce.com apply to their customers—that a reward to MVPs for providing free advocacy and service is the chance to provide *more* advocacy and service.

Table 2.2 Roles Customers Could Play in Your Business

What roles could customers play in our business?	Design or Customize	Make and Deliver	Refer, Review, Choose, Buy	Use and Maintain	Sell, Give, or Dispose of
What are our objectives, and how will we measure success?	Discovering new customer needs, promoting innovation, reducing inventory obsolescence	Reducing cost, enhancing customer relationships	Leveraging word-of mouth advertising, matching products to customer needs	Improving the customer experience, reducing technical support and service costs	Improving sustainability and resale value, creating more reasons to buy
What's in it for the customer?	A creative outlet, the ability to get exactly what he or she wants	Lower prices, the fun of producing something	Sharing their views on products with others	Being seen as an expert; documenting what he or she has learned in using the product	Feeling good about reselling or recycling the product and about upgrading
What structure or processes should we put in place to enable customers to engage? (Examples)	**Dell's** IdeaStorm groups and prioritizes tens of thousands of customer feature requests. **Walmart's** "Get It on the Shelf" program allows individuals and businesses to submit product ideas; customers vote on which ones they would like Walmart to carry.	**IKEA** makes it fun and easy for customers to assemble their own furniture, thereby enabling very low prices. **Belkin's** Wemo product, combined with the "If This, Then That" app, allows customers to create their own smart home solutions.	**American Standard, Dell,** and countless others take advantage of customer-created video demos, tutorials, and reviews of their products. **Salesforce.com** and others hold "live" events such as user conferences and workshops, in which customers rub shoulders, evangelize, and share ideas.	**Google, Microsoft, Livescribe, Salesforce.com,** and others rely on user-generated content for technical support.	**Best Buy** accepts "just about anything electronic" for recycling in its stores. **Staples** buys back used printer cartridges, and **Home Depot** recycles Christmas trees.

Clearly, putting customers to work works for Salesforce.com, and it can work for you too.

Get out of the Office and into the Field

Early in his tenure as CEO of The Home Depot, Frank Blake remarked that his nondescript appearance afforded him a huge advantage. He could "walk the stores" on the sly, observing customers, employees, and product presentation. Instead of eating lunch on the executive floor of the store support center, he was also known for descending to the employee cafeteria to sit and eat with a staff member he had not met before. Mixing with both employees and customers in this way helped Blake gain information about his business and share his thinking about the company's priorities with employees.

Blake so believes in the importance of spending time in the stores that he asks Home Depot officers to choose a team of ten employees from corporate headquarters, either from their own department or others, to work all day every Thursday in the stores, for one quarter each year. With sixty executives participating, this amounts to thousands of "manager-days" each year spent working, just as store associates do, in Home Depot locations all over the country. Blake tells corporate managers, "Don't leave a list; take a list" when visiting the stores. In other words, if you see something that needs fixing when you're working in a store, get in touch with the right person back at corporate headquarters—and see that it gets fixed.

"Frank Blake made it cool for corporate managers to spend time in the stores," says Dwaine Kimmet, treasurer and vice president of financial services for The Home Depot. Kimmet has developed an effective process for selecting and managing his "Spring in the Stores" team. He asks his direct reports to suggest managers from other departments who they think would be good team participants. This way, his team includes a mix of different functions, such as financial services, marketing, operations, supply chain, and learning solutions.

Kimmet holds a kickoff meeting at the beginning of the quarter, during which each team member shares one thing he or she would like to learn more deeply as a result of the twelve Thursdays he or she will spend working in the store—how merchandise is replenished, for example, or some other aspect of store operations. Setting this learning goal is essential; it focuses team members' attention while they're immersed in the hubbub of daily operations.

Kimmet's team gathers each Thursday morning at a Dunkin' Donuts near the store where they will work that day. Each week, one of the ten team members presents a project that he or she worked on that impacts the stores—for example, a supply chain or marketing project. This allows all team members to learn about projects outside their functional area.

Frank Blake follows up on these efforts by speaking with the store managers who have had employees from the corporate office working in their stores, to see how the teams are doing in engaging customers and employees.

The benefits of this program are vast. Says Kimmet, "It's sped up the loop. The interaction with customers is incredible, and very motivating. We get faster feedback on whether programs are working and how they need to be tweaked. We fix things faster." He continues, "It also breaks down the barriers between corporate functions, and builds relationships and knowledge. Occasionally, team members will actually change to a new job function as a result of the experience. They see something really exciting in another area, and want to be part of it."

The Home Depot prides itself on having skilled tradespeople manning the aisles of its stores. Therefore, company leaders who leave headquarters to spend a day in the store are seldom as well equipped as store associates are to deal with complex customer questions about plumbing, electrical, or landscaping. Regardless, immersing these decision makers in the flow of daily store operations has been invaluable for the company. Decision makers see the frustrations customers experience firsthand. Problems with store layout, product selection, out-of-stocks, financing, checkout and return processes, and delivery become very real and tangible—hard to ignore—when you can picture the face of a frustrated (or delighted) customer. Urgency increases and ingenuity kicks in when you are fixing a problem for a specific person instead of an invisible, nameless customer.

As a result of this experience in the field, Home Depot decision makers know how things really work in their stores. When they get back to their desks at the corporate office, they can then develop practical solutions and improvements that will work across two thousand stores and four hundred thousand employees, seven days a week.

There's no doubt that this habit of getting out into the stores to see through both the customers' and the frontline employees' eyes has paid off. As illustrated in Figure 2.1, The Home Depot's stock price has advanced 26 percent annually over the last five years, compared to 15 percent for the Standard & Poor's 500 stock index and 16 percent for its primary competitor, Lowe's.

Similarly, the management team at Delta Air Lines believes in the importance of immersing themselves in their airline's daily operations. Top Delta leaders who work at the Atlanta headquarters are each assigned to a city that Delta services. They work in this "station" a few days each year, side by side with gate agents and flight attendants. Working on the front line gives management a conduit for two-way communication and uncovers opportunities to improve operations. Maintaining this intimate interface with both customers and the front line has been essential to Delta's successful navigation through its 2005 bankruptcy and subsequent merger with Northwest Airlines in 2008, and through to its emergence as one of the world's best-performing airlines today. Delta now leads the network airlines in financial performance, and was

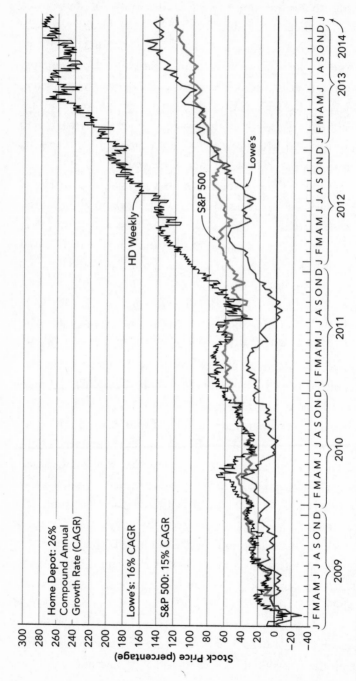

Figure 2.1 Changes in Stock Price, January 2009 to January 2014, Home Depot vs. Lowe's

named in the top fifty of *Fortune's* 2014 World's Most Admired Companies list.

These companies' habit of getting out in the field to see for themselves what new opportunities—and problems—are developing has paid off. Getting executives out of their offices and into stores, airports, and other locations creates keen market awareness. It guides leaders in making sound decisions and exposes them to market change where it's happening, as it's happening.

Even the time-honored concept of *headquarters* is becoming passé as companies such as Halliburton, Accenture, and Lenovo all have made the decision to set up several different headquarters locations for their businesses, spreading top executives among several different geographies. A person working in Belgium may supervise a staff in Africa and report to a person in Asia. For example, Lenovo's highest-level management team is spread between Singapore, North Carolina, Hong Kong, Seattle, and India. The company's top twenty leaders meet monthly, each time in a different place. These approaches help keep companies from developing tunnel vision in a single market, and give them on-the-ground experiences with the customers, cultures, and economies they serve.

Companies like Procter & Gamble (P&G) have learned to apply their core knowledge—such as insights into women's needs—and have retained their scale advantages, while adapting to and serving diverse cultures around the world. CEO A. G. Lafley is credited with resurrecting P&G after a major downturn, relaunching Olay as a high-end product line, and shepherding P&G into the men's market for the first time with the acquisition of Gillette. Every time Lafley visited a country, he went into retail stores and consumers' homes to ask questions about how people used P&G's products and whether or not they were delighted. Back at the company's Cincinnati headquarters, when he recounted these firsthand stories about the people he met and the lives they lived, it boosted commitment and inspired employees there to help grow sales in these international markets.

Give Customers a Reason to Talk, Then Listen In

Listening in on customer conversations provides valuable insight into how customer needs are evolving—and allows you to uncover opportunities the competition may never see.

Owners' groups, live events, and online communities are great places for you to learn about your customers. For example, in Cooper Mini car clubs located worldwide, owners get together for drives through the mountains, road rallies, cookouts, drive-in movie nights, and just showing off their cars. Mini enthusiasts also frequent online communities to trade tips on maintenance, modifications, choosing the right Mini model, and other brand-specific issues.

These kinds of forums increase customer loyalty and word-of-mouth marketing, and can create a virtuous cycle of customers energizing one another about your brand. They are also great places to listen in to learn about how your customers are changing and what they would like to see from your brand in the future.

Amazon creates a rich environment for sellers to share their ideas on its seller forums. No doubt someone at Amazon is paying attention to comments like this one from a business owner who sells through Amazon: "I am having the worst time listing new inventory and trying to put it under the correct and lowest number, because the new layout is so much more difficult. Any tips? Anyone else agree?"[4]

A forum for customers to share their frustrations, worries, desires, innovations, and successes can certainly serve as a window into their needs, but what if they say something negative, causing damage to your reputation and brand? Although this is a valid concern, the reverse is often the case. Apple is well known for its passionate followers, a large number of whom regularly post on Apple's Support Communities online forum (https://discussions.apple.com). These Apple-sponsored and -operated forums allow anyone to ask questions about the company's products, troubleshoot issues, look for solutions to problems, show off his latest acquisitions—and wax poetic about his love for everything Apple. Although there is plenty of griping about Apple in the forums, comments are overwhelmingly positive. Let customers say what they want, get them talking to each other, and learn from what they say.

Encourage the Unexpected

Bank of America, FedEx, IBM, USAA, and others enlist corporate clients in advisory councils, and many technology companies, including Fiserv, Salesforce.com, ESRI, and others, hold high-energy, content-filled user conferences. When a customer looks an employee in the eye and shares his frustrations, successes, and future plans, the employee cares far more and is affected more deeply than when she is reading market research reports presenting reams of dry data detailing these frustrations. Employees feel more energized to take action when a real, live human being needs their help.

User conferences are great for brand-building and customer-training purposes, but what can they do to enhance your agility? The key is to design the conference to allow—better yet, to *encourage*—the unexpected, and prepare to be surprised.

Geographic information systems company ESRI hosts more than fifteen thousand users at its San Diego user conference each July. ESRI counts among its customers government agencies, health departments, NGOs, insurance companies, retailers, restaurant chains, real estate companies, logistics companies, and other businesses from all around the world—more than 350,000 organizations in all.

Two events within the conference are particularly geared to revealing new insights about how customers are using ESRI's products. The first, the Managers Open Summit, is an "unconference" event. Rather than prescreening speakers and defining presentation topics months in advance (as do planners of most large, professional conferences), ESRI allows customers to propose topics when they arrive at the event, and any attendee wishing to learn about that topic may join in that session. This format encourages customers to spontaneously raise issues and share ideas that ESRI may not have thought of on its own.

Another session at the ESRI user conference consists of "lightning talks." Customers take five minutes to share one great idea or to tell a story that might inform, motivate, and inspire other customers. ESRI creates urgency ("Hurry and sign up!") by making only eighteen slots available. Lightning talks are a fun, easy way for customers to educate each other about new techniques for using ESRI products. Luckily, geographers are a pretty enthusiastic bunch; they truly love solving business and societal problems through clever applications of mapping software. Nothing excites them more than sharing ideas and discussing problem-solving processes and solutions.

Wikimedia, perhaps the king of crowdsourcing, hosts an Idea-Lab brainstorming session at its annual conference, which occurs at a different location each year, from Hong Kong to London. According to the event website, a typical attendee might be a "Big dreamer, details focuser, writer, designer, community organizer, project planner, developer," or a "generally awesome Wikimedia volunteer."[5] Although the invitation list is intentionally broad, the people most likely to attend this conference are Wikipedia customers and users who are most involved and invested in it. They have the greatest passion for Wikipedia's mission, and the most energy to invest in improving the platform. Wikimedia's aim is to connect people and ideas to collaboratively develop new project plans or even to initiate grants to support those projects to completion. By cultivating customer-to-customer interactions by way of the IdeaLab brainstorm, Wikimedia is highly likely to end up with a number of suggestions for improvement.

The next time you gather your customer community, set aside time for spontaneous customer presentations to stir the pot. You'll learn more about your customers' needs and about how they are using your products. And you'll build customer loyalty by prompting customers to feel that they had a hand in steering your strategy.

In Conclusion

Getting customers involved in your business, using your own and competitors' products as a customer would, and spending time in the field enable you to spot changes in your marketplace and respond to them quickly.

- **Experience what your customers do, firsthand.** Use your own and your competitors' products to discover how you can create more value for your customers.
- **Put customers to work.** Get customers involved in product development, technical support, sales, and marketing. They can often perform these roles in a lower-cost, higher-quality way than can employees—and doing so will uncover new ideas and insights.
- **Get out of the office and into the field.** Spending time in the field helps leaders see firsthand the frustrations that both customers and employees experience. It exposes them to market change as it's happening, and enables them to better identify operational improvement opportunities and innovation ideas.
- **Give customers a reason to talk, then listen in.** Owners' groups, gatherings, and online forums create a ripe environment for customers to share their frustrations, worries, desires, innovations, and successes. Listening in on these conversations provides insight on how customer needs are evolving, uncovering opportunities that the competition may never see.

- **Encourage the unexpected.** Set aside time for spontaneous customer presentations at live events, such as advisory councils, user conferences, and the like. When you encourage the unexpected, you'll learn even more about your customers' needs and how you can serve them.

Chapter Three

Right Customers, Right Value, Right Time

Identify Your Most Attractive Customers and Pivot with Them

In 1987, Howard Schultz bought the six-store Starbucks chain from the original owners, and quickly began to expand. Although that particular period during the late 1980s might not have seemed the best time to buy a chain of coffee stores—total coffee sales in the United States had fallen throughout the prior decade—Schultz saw things differently. He noticed that sales of *specialty* coffee had increased, from only 3 percent of the market in 1983 to 10 percent in 1989. He therefore chose not to focus on the 90 percent of people who, at that time, drank run-of-the-mill coffee—brewed at home or purchased for a dollar or so per cup. Instead, he capitalized on the trend that few others had spotted by catering to affluent, well-educated, primarily white-collar patrons who wanted a rich, intense, dark-roast coffee.

Schultz also saw something else that few others saw: the opportunity to create a "third place"—not home, not work—where people could spend time.[1] As he explains,

The idea was to create a chain of coffeehouses that would become America's "third place." At the time, most Americans had two places in their lives—home and work. But I believed that people needed another place, a place where they could go to relax and enjoy others, or just be by themselves. I envisioned a place that would be separate from home or work, a place that would mean different things to different people.

With this goal in mind, Schultz led Starbucks to create the coffeehouse culture in the United States and then spread that culture to sixty other countries. From its inception, Starbucks became a place for meetings, studying, relaxing, and socializing, whose equivalent had never existed before. The rise of the freelance workforce was well matched to this trend, as thousands of independent workers in each city benefited from having a reliable place to gather—and even, from time to time, to work, taking advantage of the free Wi-Fi and comfortable surroundings. Starbucks welcomes people to linger for hours in its now more than nineteen thousand stores,[2] and somehow it has made the economics work. The company's 2013 operating income was $2.5 billion on revenues of $14.9 billion.[3]

But, ultimately, it was all about the coffee—at least in the beginning. Starbucks succeeded in getting a lot of people hooked on the intense flavors, high quality, and heavy doses of caffeine. By 2014, almost as many people (34 percent) drank gourmet coffee daily as those who drank nongourmet coffee (35 percent).[4] A great measure of the growth in gourmet coffee popularity is clearly attributable to Starbucks; without its push into the gourmet coffee segment, it's unlikely that the segment would have grown to this level.

But, like that of any other fast-growing company, Starbucks' road to success has not been without its bumps. Until 2010, the company flourished via its strategy of rapidly opening new stores—often resulting in multiple Starbucks stores within just blocks of one another. (There are 255 Starbucks stores in New York City alone.[5]) After setting a goal of opening thirty thousand stores around the world, Starbucks was opening *seven* new stores every day by 2007. But then the Great Recession arrived, and the company—like most other purveyors of discretionary products—felt the ill effects on its bottom line. By 2010, Starbucks had retrenched, closing almost nine hundred stores and letting more than thirty-four thousand employees go.[6]

As the economy has gradually recovered, Starbucks has implemented a new, three-part strategy for revitalizing growth by gaining new customers while creating added value for current customers:

- **Attract new coffee customers.** Starbucks has already begun aggressively implementing this element of the strategy, most notably by expanding beyond its historical core market of dark-roast coffee lovers. In 2012, the company introduced a new line of light-roast coffee under the Blonde Roast label, targeted at the 40 percent of customers who prefer a lighter roast than the company's typical dark offerings. The strategy has shown promise, with Starbucks reporting that Blonde Roast packaged coffee sales showed 79 percent incremental growth in grocery stores and 70 percent at Starbucks retail stores in 2012.[7]
- **Offer new value for core dark-roast customers.** To improve the coffee experience for its core customers, the coffee connoisseurs, Starbucks has introduced the expensive Clover brewing system to a limited number of stores. This system uses vacuum-press technology, precise digital temperature control, and a special filter to allow Starbucks customers to "discover new layers and dimensions" in their coffee. Starbucks has paired this machine with a limited quantity of the very best coffee beans the company can acquire from around the world, which are unavailable to its regular, non-Clover customers.

- **Add new products and new markets.** Likely observing the strong interest of its core clientele in health and wellness, and seeking to grow within the $50 billion health-and-wellness market, Starbucks has created what Schultz describes as a "brand-new retail concept around health and wellness that's never been done before."[8] In 2011, Starbucks acquired the little-known Evolution Fresh brand, and just four months later began to open Evolution Fresh juice stores—its first store concept that does not revolve around coffee.

  The juice is cold-pressed in a central facility, then flows out of eight taps in the store. A range of salads, "bowls," and wraps, including vegan options, round out the product offering. If this foray into health and wellness is successful, Starbucks may create a new cultural phenomenon, as it did in building the coffeehouse culture years ago.

When prioritizing growth initiatives, it is helpful to strike a balance between developing new products and aiming at new markets. Figure 3.1 shows Starbucks growth initiatives, as I would plot them, in terms of the degree to which the company is stepping out of its traditional product/market box. One initiative—the foray into health-and-wellness stores—is to some extent both a new product and a new market for Starbucks. Although this top right box is the riskiest to play in, Starbucks has minimized this risk, as it is expert both at running retail businesses and at creating new demand for and culture around high-priced specialty beverages. This endeavor, then, is a moderate and well-thought-out step into new products and new markets.

At the same time that Starbucks is advancing into new territory, it is careful to continually enhance the brand experience for its core customers. The Clover coffee machine takes an existing product to its existing customers, thus putting it in the bottom left box of Figure 3.1. It creates a distinctive and differentiated dark-roast coffee taste and experience, which will be difficult and

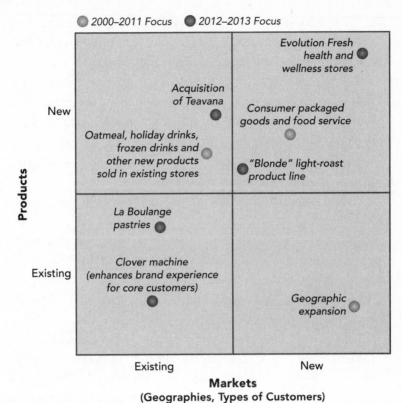

Figure 3.1 Starbucks Expansion Initiatives

expensive for competitors to match. This balance of aggressive expansion and moderated risk has served Starbucks well, and enables agility in the face of fast-changing market conditions.

In 1995, a year before Starbucks opened its first international location in Tokyo, I worked with Malaysian luxury retailer Melium to help introduce the café culture to Malaysia by opening the first Dome Café in Kuala Lumpur. As a former British colony, and with mountaintop tea plantations, Malaysia is a tea-drinking country; its per-capita tea consumption is about two-and-a-half times the United States level.[9] The Malaysians often mix copious amounts of sweetened condensed milk with their tea, making a thick, sweet concoction.

The Malaysian retail market was booming in the mid-1990s, with new, upscale malls being built at an astounding rate. Melium founder and owner Dato' Farah Khan and I met with the developers of each mall, who each gave us their spiel on how many square feet they were planning, the water features and kids' attractions they were installing, and why Melium's high-end brands—which included Ermenegildo Zegna, Thierry Mugler, Hugo Boss, and Aigner, in addition to Dome Café—would be the perfect fit for their locale and demographics.

Dato' Farah Khan didn't worry that the GDP per capita in Malaysia was only about $4,600 at the time.[10] As a brilliant businesswoman, Khan knew that there was a market for an international and upscale lifestyle among a certain growing slice of the Malaysian population, and that visitors from Japan and other luxury-goods-loving cultures would buy her fashionable brands and experience.

Khan's excellent business instincts and superb execution have paid off. Both Dome Café and the apparel businesses have grown healthily for two decades. The Farah Khan brand, designed by Khan herself, has become an international success, worn by stars and sold in over seventy cities worldwide, including Milan, Paris, São Paulo, and New York. As an *Edge* newspaper article profiling Khan reported in 2009, "She has an innate ability to catch waves of opportunity as they roll by."[11]

Howard Schultz and Farah Khan teach us that we can enhance our agility by focusing on a small but growing group of highly attractive customers who may be very different from the "average" customer. If you try to understand and respond to *all* customers, you are unlikely to provide compelling, market-share-winning value for any of them. Only by narrowing your focus can you intimately understand your customers' needs and desires. And by focusing your talent, creativity, management attention, and investments on a specific, attractive portion of the market, you are more likely to succeed in winning that market.

So what do you do after you have already satisfied this initial group of highly attractive customers, and competitors are beginning to copy your offering?

That's where agility comes in.

When Starbucks realized that it was already earning near-maximum profit from its historical base of dark-roast coffee connoisseurs, it continued to invest to protect and delight this high-margin group of customers by introducing the Clover machine. When it looked for growth, it noticed the opportunity to sell to a new group of customers: the 40 percent of Americans who prefer light-roast coffee. Looking even farther outside of its historical core focus, it also saw an opportunity to penetrate an entirely new group of customers who are looking for a new health-and-wellness experience, creating the Evolution Fresh store in response.

Your Customers Can Show You the Way

Investing in products and markets that are already doing well is an obvious opportunity, yet many companies do not know which customers (or customer segments) and products are growing the fastest or which are most profitable to serve.

When companies examine their profit by customer or customer segment, they often see a picture like Figure 3.2. A few customers drive more than 80 percent of the profit, a large number of customers are barely profitable to serve, and a few customers are unprofitable to serve. The "flat spot" in the middle of the graph typically reflects customers who do not view the offering as differentiated (or who are buying the company's more commoditized products). These customers choose vendors based largely on price; as a result, the company's profits are slim.

When looking at profitability by customer or by customer segment, ask yourself these questions:

- How can we sell more to our most profitable customers, on the left side of the graph—and attract more customers like this?

If they are buying different products than the average customer, how can we bring out more products that are similarly
differentiated? How can we introduce these differentiated
products to more customers who would value them?

- What can we do to improve profits in the more commoditized
  portion of our business (the middle of the graph)? Can we offer
  any add-on services to earn additional revenue? For example,
  an airline can offer a more comfortable economy-class seat for
  a moderate up-charge. Are there ways we can take cost out
  of the equation without diminishing important value for the
  customer—or better yet, while simultaneously *increasing* customer value? For example, when airlines automate passenger
  check-in or streamline the rebooking of passengers after flight
  cancellations, they simultaneously reduce cost and improve
  the customer experience.

- What can we do to improve profitability on the right side of
  the graph—those customers on whom we lose money? Can we
  eliminate costs or raise prices? What would be the real, incremental impact on profits if we lost these customers? Should
  we take steps to stop serving them, such as eliminating sales
  calls to them?

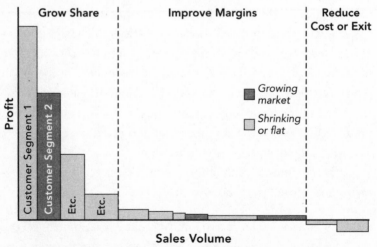

Figure 3.2 Profit and Volume by Customer Segment

Assess Growth and Profitability by Customer

Gathering the data to create a chart like Figure 3.2 is easy for companies that have strong financial systems with robust business intelligence tools. However, it can often be difficult for companies to gather and understand this data. Customer data may be spread across many orders, divisions, and geographies, and a variety of products—meaning that there's no easy way to gather sales by customer. Tangled and disjointed information systems—often the result of growing through acquisition—compound this problem and can make it difficult to assess sales and profit data at the customer segment or product level.

Profitability data is more challenging to assemble than sales data, as many companies do not allocate costs to specific customers and products. In addition, there are many different valid ways of allocating costs, depending on the question you are trying to answer.

When you encounter these problems, look for a simple and expedient way to identify profitable and growing products and customer segments. Do a quick analysis using a snapshot or "time slice" of data, or when all else fails, ask four or five knowledgeable managers to independently estimate profitability by customer group. If they all agree, you have succeeded in generating at least a first-pass assessment of sales growth and profitability by customer. (Be careful, though; instincts can be misleading in this area.)

In summary, figure out what reasonably accurate and fast-to-assemble data you *can* get. Don't worry if it's not perfect or if it's incomplete—at least for the first pass. Some data is far better than no data at all. You can start a conversation about what strategies to take to fix the situation, and then refine the data before making any irrevocable decisions.

When You See Fast Growth or High Profitability, Find Out What's Behind It

Once you've identified your most profitable and fastest-growing customers, then seek to understand *why*. Are certain customers or market segments paying a higher price? If so, *why* is this individual—or group—willing to pay more? Does your product create more value for them than for other customers? If so, figure out how you can find and attract more customers who see this value.

If a certain customer group is less costly to serve than others, then find out why. Is it because these customers don't insist on rush shipments as often or because they need less service? Do they buy a very standard product that you can make very efficiently? Once you understand why certain customers are less costly to serve, figure out how to attract more customers like them, or how you can influence the other customers to behave more like them.

Likewise, understand why fast-growing customers are buying more each year. The "why" can often lead to surprising insights and opportunities. Is *their* end-user market growing? That is, are your customers' customers buying more than they used to? Has your competitor faltered in the market where they reside? Have any unusual conditions in their geographic area—such as new tax policies, a boom in construction, or weather events—caused a spike in sales? Learn from your successes, and expand or replicate the actions you took to win these customers. Shift resources to focus on attracting more customers like them.

Look for Customers Who Are Using Your Products in an Unusual Way

If you see customers who are using your product or service in an unusual way—or using your product more often—you may have struck gold. Once you get to the bottom of it, figure out what you can do to get the word out about this new way of using the product to attract more customers like them.

Navigation company Garmin Ltd. has done a good job of developing new product and product-enhancement ideas by observing how customers use its products. Proliferating smart-phone GPS apps and the inclusion of OEM navigation systems in automobiles have caused the company's sales in its biggest

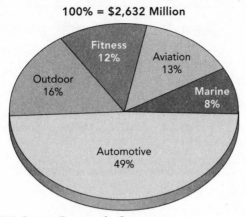

100% = $2,632 Million

Figure 3.3 2013 Garmin Revenue by Segment
Source: Garmin Ltd., *2013 Annual Report*, http://sites.garmin.com/annualreport/.

market segment, automotive (49 percent of sales, as shown in Figure 3.3), to decline 10 percent annually since 2011,[12] driving the need to find new sources of growth.

Although Garmin is gaining share in the personal navigation device market, the market overall is shrinking.[13] Garmin knows that it has to gain share in specialty GPS markets other than automotive in order to combat this trend. The company has therefore invested heavily in innovation, growing R&D from 10 percent of sales in 2010 to 14 percent of sales in 2013. It has the luxury of carrying no debt and retaining healthy profits (net income was 23 percent of sales in 2013), despite the decline in sales. The R&D focus is both to grow sales in nonautomotive markets and to increase the value for motorists, relative to smartphone applications, such as Google Maps.

The payoff of this innovation effort has been healthy growth in fitness, outdoor, and aviation, which has partly mitigated Garmin's revenue decline in the automotive market. Figure 3.4 shows the revenue growth and loss for each of the company's key customer segments.

Garmin watched what users did with its products, even if the products were not designed for that use. It sought to understand each market segment's specialized needs, then innovated to serve

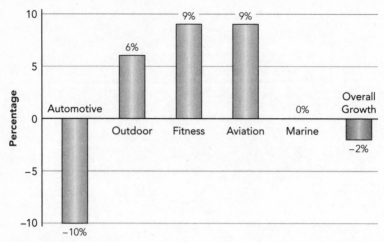

Figure 3.4 Garmin Revenue, Compound Annual Growth Rate, by Segment, 2011 to 2013

Source: Garmin Ltd., "Financial Review," *2013 Annual Report,* http://sites.garmin.com /annualreport/.

those needs. Each year, for example, Garmin adds new specialty models catering to different sports. The golf model, which features thirty thousand preloaded courses, keeps track of a golfer's average yardage with each club. The swimming model counts strokes and laps, and can even detect what kind of stroke (freestyle, butterfly, and so on) the user is swimming. Some running models offer heart rate monitoring and calorie consumption, and allow runners to upload and share their workout data. Cycling models offer speed, distance, altitude, and calories-burned functions, plus real-time connectivity through a smartphone, which allows live tracking, social media sharing, and weather updates. Consumers use Garmin's outdoor products for hiking, hunting, backpacking, and even tracking and training search-and-rescue and police dogs. The brand's Tactix watch was designed with military special operations in mind. Marine models offer autopilot, fish finding, and other specialized features.

This innovation and investment in catering to the specialized needs of each market segment has helped Garmin stay ahead of the barrage of specialized mobile apps targeted at these same markets—not to mention offerings from competitors, such as Nike in fitness, Raymarine in marine, and Honeywell in aviation. As a result, Garmin has mitigated declining sales in the automotive market with growth in other market segments.

Examine the market segments you serve, and learn from customers who are using your products in new and innovative ways. These customers will help you to make smart investments to stay ahead of the competitive pack.

Direct Resources Toward Your Most Attractive Customers

No company has infinite capacity to serve all customers as they might love to be served. Therefore, you need to consider how you can allocate your scarce resources toward your most profitable customers and the customer groups that you can grow the fastest.

An industrial products company, for example, might decide that it should flag its most profitable and attractive customers in its order management and customer relationship management systems. This would allow the company to treat these customers to a variety of perks, such as:

- More frequent visits from salespeople, or from more highly skilled salespeople
- Preferred access to engineering assistance, quarterly visits, or a technical support hotline
- Designated inside sales personnel and faster turnaround on quotations
- Shorter lead times in manufacturing, or waived fees when an order has to be expedited
- Dedicated inventory
- First notice of new products, or exclusive access to new products
- The opportunity to collaborate on development of new products

- More integration of order management systems
- Access to special online resources
- Volume rebates
- Annual visits from top company leaders

Think about how you can cater to your best customers to attract more of their business.

Your Products Can Show You the Way

Just as you looked at high-profit, fast-growth customers to determine where to focus your resources, you also want to look at *products* that are especially high profit or that have fast-growing sales—and figure out why by asking:

- What's special about them?
- Who is using them?
- Should you introduce more products in that line or get the word out to more customers about that product's value?

As in the "customer" analysis described in the previous section, looking at aberrations in product growth rates and profitability can reveal changes in the marketplace and new opportunities.

Market Share as an Indicator of Opportunity

Observing which of your product lines and customer segments have a higher market share can yield insights that are hard to gain from profitability and revenue growth information alone. When specialty chemical manufacturer Cabot Corporation performed an analysis of market share by product, the company came to some very surprising conclusions. Cabot manufactured a specialty chemical called carbon black, which it sold to Goodyear, Michelin, and other major tire companies. Company managers needed to improve profitability, yet their products were largely undifferentiated from those of other carbon black manufacturers, such as J. M. Huber. As a result, tough procurement negotiators viewed them as a commodity vendor, and Cabot's salespeople had little backbone when pressured to drop price—which they inevitably did.

Yet Cabot's market share analysis revealed that while market share for most of the company's carbon black products was roughly 30 percent, a product used in truck tires called Regal 300 enjoyed more than *double* Cabot's average market share—over 60 percent. Cabot had to use some creative approaches to obtain these market share numbers—including such techniques as counting the customer plants served, the number of plants served by competitors, and tons of product consumed at each.

Sensing an opportunity, Cabot asked customers what they liked about the product that was capturing such a large market share. The company learned that tires using Regal 300 could be retreaded far more times than tires using competitive products, with fewer retread failures. If you've seen tread flying off a truck tire at freeway speed, you know how important Regal 300 was to highway safety. Happily, Cabot found that it could raise this valuable, differentiated product's price with little pushback from tire company customers.

The Magic Matrix: Looking at Product and Customer Performance Simultaneously

Harvard Business School professor Ben Shapiro has a name for looking simultaneously across both customer segments and products to examine profitability, growth, and market share. He calls it the "magic matrix."

Note that even without investing in the time to develop highly accurate data, you can often come up with an intelligent guess at which combinations of products and customers are most attractive, which are least attractive, and which are somewhere in the middle. Once you've done this, you can begin to think creatively about how to grow those most attractive customer segments and products. You might even chose to walk away from certain customer segments and products if you can't improve profitability.

Segment Customers According to *Why* They Are Using Your Products

My needs as a business traveler are very different from my needs as a leisure traveler. Frequency and schedule of flights are very important when I fly for business—so I am willing to pay a higher price to get these. Three other family members often accompany me when I'm traveling for leisure, so low prices, in-flight entertainment, and seat configuration are more important to me in that scenario.

Therefore, airlines should not "average" my business and leisure needs if they want to develop insight into my customer preferences. Rather, they should look at each of these travel circumstances as a distinct case.

Just as Farah Khan would not have been well served to look at the average income per capita in Malaysia, looking at your average customer is unlikely to reveal many opportunities. Viewing your customers segment by segment, however, will uncover a great deal. Dividing customers on the basis of *why* or even *when* they are using your products will yield the maximum insight into customer needs and what customers will buy in the future.

Niches and Microcultures Reveal New Opportunities for Growth

If your company is among the first to spot and cater to growing niche markets with specialized needs, you can easily establish a differentiated and lucrative offering. Consider dog clothing—an unknown market just ten years ago that is now one of PetSmart's and Petco's fastest-growing and most profitable product lines. The 2011–2012 American Pet Products Association's National Pet

Owners Survey reveals that despite the sluggish economy, spending on treats, toys, and accessories for dogs was up 30 percent in 2010—and that 10 percent of dog owners reported having "hosted parties for their dogs."[14] PetSmart capitalizes on these trends by selling merchandise like Halloween toys and costumes for dogs and by targeting niche market segments such as gay pet owners and second-generation Hispanic customers.[15] These niches not only provide new opportunities for profitable growth but also often presage important changes in the broader market.

Observe "Outlier" Customers

It's easy for organizations to be lulled to sleep by the rhythms of daily operations—the same types of customers, buying the same products, using them in the same way, day after day. Observing "outlier" customers, however, can do wonders for an organization's agility and creativity. Customers who are using your product or service in an unusual way can be a harbinger of things to come.

Outliers are customers who

- Use your product in an unusual way, under extreme conditions
- Seem to get unusual value from your product or service (often, but not always, indicated by higher margins)
- Have gone to extra trouble to acquire your product, or have surmounted an obstacle to use it
- Need much less *or* much more service and attention than average
- Are achieving fast growth
- Are struggling or are losing market share (especially if your product may be able to help)
- Operate in a particularly risky or fast-changing industry
- Modify or combine your product with another, or use only a part of your product
- Add value to your product and resell it

- Are using your product in a geography or market that your sales channel does not serve
- Are particularly innovative and forward thinking, or are trendsetters

For example: when trying to optimize the range of a several-year-old Cisco wireless router at our lake house, my husband stumbled on the story of some people in Africa who had modified the same unit by adding a more powerful power supply. As a result, they'd succeeded in extending the Wi-Fi range to *192 miles*. (We only needed it to reach our dock!) When seeking to generate ideas for product innovation, Cisco might look at examples of such customers who have made its products do amazing things.

Market research and management reporting systems tend to "average" all customers together, blending specific needs into a bland summary of generalized information. As a result, we lose valuable insights about customer needs. In contrast, identifying and observing outliers can help you generate ideas for new products, markets, channels, and product modifications and enhancements. This process can also uncover opportunities to take value out of your offerings—thereby reducing cost often without impacting customer satisfaction.

Continuous Customer Intelligence: Harnessing Data to Gain Up-to-the-Minute Foresight

Data from social media, Web, and mobile interactions; sensors; transactions; and other sources is being generated at an astounding rate. Every day, we create 2.5 quintillion bytes of data, and 90 percent of all data ever created has been produced in the last two years.[16] Luckily, it seems that new software tools are also designed every month to make sense of the data—allowing us to increasingly slice, dice, aggregate, and analyze this information to unlock new insights.

If utilized well, "big data" helps you to know which way the wind is blowing and to sense upcoming shifts. Techniques like text analytics and sentiment analysis enable you to process massive amounts of data to develop continuously refreshed customer insight. Retailers like Zara (based in Spain), Forever 21 (based in Korea), and H&M (based in Sweden) are expert at "reading the signals" of shifting demand. They quickly introduce new products to meet emerging demand trends, and manage inventory expertly to keep high-demand products in stock and to minimize markdowns and discounting. These companies pair data analytics with good communication between store managers, who have daily contact with customers, and designers and planners at headquarters. Zara, for instance, manufactures about ten thousand designs per year in small batches, then watches which do best—enabling the brand to move quickly when it has identified winning fashion trends, while cutting its losses quickly on unpopular items.[17]

Using analytical software tools to observe customers' behavior and values and to listen in on their conversations allows you to determine where to best deploy your resources. For example, companies gain up-to-the-minute insights on customer views, frustrations, and needs by tapping into online user forums; Amazon, TripAdvisor, and Yelp reviews; and comments on Facebook, blogs, and Twitter. Other companies gather intelligence from customer service call reports, geolocation data from mobile devices, and other operational databases.

Table 3.1 presents a framework to help your company decide how best to employ data analytics, and what steps to take to gain the right data, expertise, and technology to make continuous customer insight a reality.

Automate Customization

Advances in technology have helped to substantially reduce the cost of catering to specific customer tastes and needs. This

Table 3.1 Using Data Analytics for Innovation, Operations, and Marketing

Type of Data	Examples, by Area of Focus		
	Innovation	Operations	Marketing
Internal (company) data	Use text analytics to mine call-center reports for product enhancement ideas	Optimize production levels based on analysis of customer demand	Analyze transaction and Web data to develop cross-sell and prospecting strategies
Internal data combined with customer or channel data	Combine sales information from multiple channels to identify emerging customer trends	Trigger after-sales service by monitoring sensor data from products as they are used	Develop geotargeted mobile ads, and adjust on the fly based on customer response
Internal data combined with external data	Mine data from social media, user support forums, and reviews to discern what customers want next	Employ geolocation data from cell phones, combined with weather data, to optimize inventory in each locale	Measure customer sentiment, and tailor marketing messages in real time

opens up an important avenue for enhancing foresight. You can now experiment continuously, gathering data about how your customers respond to different offers.

For example, technology and advertising company Cardlytics enables banks to offer their credit-card holders coupons for local merchants, tailored to each cardholder's purchasing habits. These customized coupons are presented when a customer views his online account statement, and are automatically credited to his account statement when he makes a purchase, so no paper is involved. It's a win-win-win for the merchants, the banks, and the cardholder.

When I process my boarding pass for an overbooked Delta Air Lines flight, Delta presents me with a screen that asks, "Select the dollar value of the travel voucher you would accept as compensation for volunteering your seat." I can select the $50, $75, $100, or $125 level before clicking the "submit bid" button. This system not only lowers Delta's outlay for compensating volunteers on overbooked flights but also enables the airline to identify price-sensitive customers—the ones willing to change flights for $50. They might use this information to preferentially target promotions to these customers or to develop a new, lower-priced product for them, such as a ticket that enables them to fly on a certain day but only on a space-available basis.

Similarly, Delta can identify the customers who *don't* opt to volunteer at all—like me—who might be good targets for premium products or fee-based upgrades. For instance, I would be willing to pay extra to get home quicker when flights are full. This bidding process opens the door for all kinds of new revenue management and customer segmentation.

Amazon is the master of "mass customization." A significant percentage of Amazon purchases come as the result of suggestions made by the company's powerful customization software, which automatically presents customers with products they are likely to want to buy, based on their site-browsing habits and previous purchases.

Customization has two huge benefits. First, it enables a company to uniquely satisfy customer needs, which leads to healthier profit margins and higher revenues. Second, because companies can observe and quantify customer responses to varied offers, it provides insight into emerging customer preferences.

In Conclusion

Ultimately, one of the best ways to maximize revenue and profit is to provide the right customers with the right value at the right time. This chapter has discussed a variety of different ways to determine who your right customers are, what the right value is, and when the right time is. As you review your own customer segments and product offerings, keep the following points in mind:

- **Beware the curse of averages—how most customer data obscures the real story.** If Howard Schultz at Starbucks had paid attention only to the declining coffee consumption in the United States—and had not noticed nor catered to the rising consumption of specialty coffees—he would not have built Starbucks to what it is today.

- **Look for opportunities to offer new products and services to your core customers and to bring existing products to new markets.** By bringing its customers innovative and intriguing new value, like the ultra-high-end Clover coffee brewing system, Starbucks continues to dazzle its most loyal customers with the highest-quality product possible. And it brought a new, light-roast version of its existing product—coffee—to an entirely new market: the 40 percent of Americans who say they prefer light-roast coffee.

- **Shift resources toward your most profitable and fastest-growing customers and product lines.** Understand why profitable customers are willing and able to pay more for your product or why they are less costly to serve. Examine why fast-growing customer groups are buying more each year. Do they find hidden value in your product? Are *their* end-user markets growing? Find ways to expand or replicate these successes.

- **Examine niches, microcultures, and "outlier" customers to reveal new opportunities for growth.** If your company is among the first to spot and cater to growing niche markets with specialized needs, you can easily establish a differentiated and lucrative offering.

- **Gain continuous customer intelligence for an up-to-the-minute view into coming market shifts.** Data from social media, Web, and mobile interactions; sensors; transactions; and other sources is being created at an astounding rate; you can analyze this data to illuminate previously unseen or unnoticed customer trends. Use the results to determine where to allocate your resources to meet coming demand.

- **Automate customization to gain continuous customer insight.** You can learn a lot when you give customers choices and watch what they do. Experiment continuously, then observe and quantify customer responses to understand how preferences are shifting.

Chapter Four

Love the Problem
Dig Deep to Find New Insights

Joe Gebbia and Brian Chesky studied industrial design together at the Rhode Island School of Design and quit their jobs in 2008 without any idea about what to do next—except that they wanted to start a business together. Sketchbooks in hand, they had just begun to brainstorm possible business ideas when they received notice from their landlord that their rent was going up 25 percent. If they wanted to keep their San Francisco apartment, they needed money—and *fast*.[1]

It just so happened that five thousand designers were descending on San Francisco during the upcoming weekend for a major design conference, and there were not enough hotel rooms in the city to accommodate them all. Gebbia and Chesky looked at the extra floor space in their apartment, and remembered that they had an airbed stashed in a closet. Within a day, they put up a simple website offering to host visiting designers in their apartment. They bought two more airbeds, and whimsically named their weekend offering "Airbed and Breakfast."

Within a couple of days of launching their website in 2008, the Airbnb founders had confirmed three guests: 38-year-old Kat from Boston, 32-year-old Amol from India, and Michael, a 45-year-old husband and father of five from Utah. Gebbia and

Chesky picked up Kat, Amol, and Michael at the airport, and took the trio to their favorite burrito restaurant and to parties at their friends' places. They shot photos of the fun they had. As Gebbia recounts, "We did it because we needed the money, but the social interaction was actually much more valuable."

Within a few weeks, a tech-savvy friend who had also quit his job, Nate Blecharczyk, joined with Gebbia and Chesky, and the three set out to grow the fledgling business.

Just five years later, in 2013, Airbnb was operating in 192 countries and had $2.5 billion in revenues and five hundred thousand listings. More than nine million guests have stayed in an Airbnb accommodation—50,000 to 60,000 people each day. Was growing to this level smooth and easy? No; but Gebbia, Chesky, and Blecharczyk's magical mixture of ingenuity, hard work, and agility made it possible.

The Airbnb story is an exceptional illustration of how a deep understanding of customer problems and experiences can lead to breakthrough innovation and extraordinary growth.

The founders' experience of hosting their three initial guests in 2008 was the beginning of what Gebbia calls being "married to the problem." In Airbnb's case, the "problem" was how to create new sources of income for people with spare capacity in their homes, while also creating more vibrant, engaging, and immersive experiences for travelers. Airbnb created something out of nothing; the founders spotted an opportunity that no one had ever focused on before, and addressed that opportunity in a way that created new value for both hosts and guests.

The Airbnb problem is an interesting and inspiring one to solve—not only for Gebbia and Chesky but also for their hundreds of passionate employees. Airbnb now prides itself on being a leader in the "sharing economy," matching people who have extra resources with people who can use those resources. Airbnb hosts offer everything from treehouses to islands, castles, houseboats, an igloo—even space in a tent at the front of the line the night before an iPhone release (which went for $400).

Being married to the problem drives the Airbnb founders to continually listen to customers, adapt their offerings, and learn from their failures. Immediately after their small but significant success in hosting Kat, Amol, and Michael in 2008, Gebbia, Chesky, and Blecharczyk began to percolate the idea of signing up more hosts like themselves at the upcoming South by Southwest (SXSW) conference in Austin, and made plans to travel to that city. However, the conference resulted in a total of fifteen hosts, but just two reservations—one of which was made by the Airbnb founders. In purely economic terms, the result was a failure. However, experiencing Airbnb from the guest's perspective gave them new insights on the problem they were setting out to solve.

Airbnb next focused on signing up hosts and guests for the 2008 Democratic National Convention in Denver. The convention presented a unique opportunity for Airbnb problem solving: seventy-five thousand people were expected to visit Denver for Barack Obama's speech at the Mile High Stadium, but the city had only forty thousand hotel rooms. Airbnb began to talk to local bloggers about their offering, and before they knew it, CNN was asking for an interview—and ABC, CBS, NBC, the *Guardian* in London, and *La Monde* in Paris covered the story. The surge in publicity caused Airbnb's Denver revenues to soar. Immediately after the convention, however, Airbnb encountered what Gebbia calls "the Midwest of Analytics"—revenues flattened to only $200 per week for eight months, which wasn't even enough for rent.

Anxious to stop funding the company on their credit cards and passionate about building a company together, the founders posted a graph showing weekly revenue on their bathroom mirror, and set the goal of generating $1,000 per week. While this was a laughably small amount by Silicon Valley standards, the three calculated that this amount would be enough to cover rent and ramen noodles. As Gebbia says, "You have unlimited runway if you are happy with that lifestyle."

The founders realized that if they were going to create a moneymaking business, they needed to develop a deeper understanding of host needs. To do this, they traveled to New York City, Chicago, Miami, Portland, and other cities to hold "meet-ups" with potential hosts—who, despite infrequent bookings, *seemed* to be doing everything right. The on-the-ground visits to these cities, however, highlighted a major gap in the way Airbnb was presenting the listings. The hosts' amateur photographs of their living spaces were dark and uninspiring, and they did a poor job of highlighting the essence and charm of their neighborhoods. To remedy this, the founders brought professional lighting and their designers' sensibility to the hosts' homes, and shot warm, inviting photos of the living spaces. The next week, revenue doubled, from $200 per week to $400 per week. Buoyed by this result, the founders began to travel to a different city each weekend, taking photos of listings and neighborhoods. The impact was immediate. Revenue doubled again and again. Visiting customers and enhancing the product was working wonders, and listings skyrocketed.

By 2011, Gebbia relates, "You could stand at almost any intersection in Manhattan, and one of the four buildings around you will have at least one Airbnb listing." Airbnb now has twenty-five hundred top-notch photographers around the world; they not only help hosts showcase their homes more effectively but also capture the essence of what makes each neighborhood unique. By 2013, over 1.7 million professional photos had been taken for the Airbnb site.

Even now that the founders are running a $2.5 billion revenue company, they remain committed to a culture of customer immersion and continuous innovation. CEO Chesky recently traveled thirty-six thousand miles, staying with fifteen different Airbnb hosts as he circumnavigated the globe. The company has opened eight international offices so that it can be close to the markets, guests, and hosts that it serves. Being married to the problem led not only to financial success but also to remarkable human impact for Airbnb.

Observe the Customers' Daily Environment, the Tools They Use, and the People They Interact With

The Airbnb story illustrates the value of digging deep to truly understand your customers' problems, and constantly innovating to address these problems in ever-improved ways. With the world's population rising and diets shifting to be more protein based, AGCO—maker of Massey Ferguson, Challenger, and other well-known agricultural equipment brands—is committed to solving a big problem: feeding the world.

As AGCO leaders noticed the availability of ever more powerful electronics technologies, they wanted to take a deep look at farmers' work and lives to determine the best ways to employ those electronics to improve farm yields, efficiency, safety, and sustainability.

Company researchers traveled to farms in Brazil, Russia, China, Africa, and elsewhere.[2] They observed each farmer and/or farm manager, shadowing him as he did his work and watching what he had trouble with, whom he interacted with, what was important to him, and what opportunities might exist to improve his efficiency and results.

The team was surprised to find that most farmers not only had smartphones but also enjoyed fairly reliable wireless connectivity—even in developing countries where other infrastructure was lacking. The company had been concerned that it would take years to roll out new electronics systems for the farmers; however, this smartphone availability created an opportunity to employ consumer electronics to which farmers already had access—and that dramatically shortened development time.

During their visits, the researchers observed problems that farmers faced managing their employees and contract workers. For example, contractors would sometimes surreptitiously "borrow" the farmer's expensive farm equipment to plow neighboring farmers' fields to make money on the side. Farmers also pointed out to researchers that some of their machinery—and workers—were far more productive than others, yet there was no easy way to replicate the operating parameters between machines.

These in-depth observations in the farmers' own environment formed the basis for a number of important AGCO innovations. First, the company created new tools that allowed farmers to use their smartphones and tablets to control, compare, and monitor their equipment remotely. For example, if one combine is more efficient than the others, the farmer can identify this and make corrections to his other machines. In addition, the new innovations allowed farmers to easily transfer productivity and operating data to decision support and service providers, thereby allowing those providers to make recommendations to improve yields and efficiency. Farmers can also pass data to suppliers of seeds, fertilizers, and other chemicals, in order to more accurately specify the right products and quantities. They can share information with insurers so as to purchase the right insurance at the right price. And, in the future, they can have equipment diagnosed and serviced remotely to reduce costly visits from service people.

The AGCO research was particularly valuable because the company took an in-depth, on-the-ground view of changes and opportunities throughout the farmers' entire ecosystem—the set of businesses and people with whom farmers interact. Although this approach is critical when working in business-to-business markets, it can also be valuable in consumer markets. For example, in considering the launch of a new product, Coca-Cola thinks not just about its product's *consumer*—say, the teenager—but also about the *purchaser* (Mom or Dad), the retail and food service

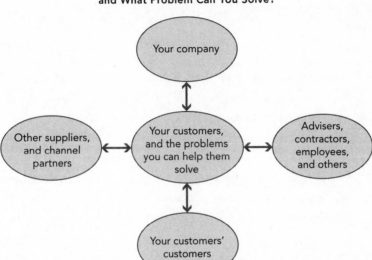

What Is Changing in Your Customer's Ecosystem, and What Problem Can You Solve?

Figure 4.1 Your Customer's Ecosystem

establishments that will sell the product, and the local bottler. Coca-Cola managers will even shadow merchandisers to make sure they stock new product on the shelves effectively.[3]

Figure 4.1 is a thought-starter for listing the different entities you might think about in your business. Who are the players that influence how your customer experiences your product or service and how her problem gets solved?

Observe and Interview Customers to Identify Opportunities in Business-to-Business Markets

Observing and talking to the customer and players in a business-to-business customer's ecosystem will help you spot changes, emerging needs, and opportunities. Consider the following approaches, taking into account your specific situation.

What to Observe

Watch customers in their natural context, such as in their work-places, and be sure to

- **Examine the *entire process*.** Follow your product through as the customer receives and uses it. Watch how the different players in the customer's business experience your service. What is changing in their process or needs? What new problems and opportunities do these changes create?
- **Observe how people use your *competitor's* products and services.** Note how the customer's experience using the competitor's product contrasts with his or her experience using yours. Does your product solve a different problem than your competitor's does? Does it solve the same problem in a different way? Have you made the most of any advantage you have—and communicated these differences to customers?
- **Watch what happens *before, during,* and *after* the time that your product or service is employed.** Do problems occur upstream or downstream that your product or service could help to solve? What triggers the need for your product? Could you solve the customer's problem earlier, or prevent it altogether?
- **Witness the customer process during *both their busy and their slow times*.** Is there anything that could be optimized to make your offering more useful, easier to consume, or more effective during peak times? Is there a way to take cost out of your offering during slow times, without reducing value to the customer?
- **Look at the *tools, processes, and outside services* your customer uses in addition to those you provide.** Have any changes occurred in the tools, processes, and services your customer uses other than those you provide? How do these affect the customer problem you are solving? Are there opportunities to make your product work better with other

products? Could you partner with other service providers to offer a bundled package that is more efficient or easier to use than buying the services separately? How can you help make the other tools and processes that your customer uses more effective?

Whom to Talk To

To gather data that is both accurate and useful, you've got to be talking to the right people. Here are some tips on how to do that:

- **Understand not just decision makers but the *full spectrum* of users.** Talk to a broad range of people within your customers' organizations, not just those responsible for the purchase decision. Anyone who uses, touches, or could benefit from your product or service is fair game. You are seeking input from
  - **A variety of *functions*.** For example, observe and talk to operations, engineering, or maintenance about how they employ your product and any problems they encounter. Talk to planning and procurement about how you might enhance the ordering and delivery experience. Talk to sales and customer service about what frustrations your customers' customers are experiencing, and how your product or service might help alleviate them. Ride along with your customers' sales reps, and speak directly with your customers' customers if possible.
  - **A variety of *layers*.** For example, talk to executives, middle management, and the front line. Executives can give you an excellent perspective on the big picture: how your product could enhance their company's competitive advantage, what changes are taking place in the marketplace, and what they would like you to innovate next to fuel their success. Middle management is often the best source for metrics and process improvement ideas. These

individuals are equipped to tell you how your delivery performance is trending or how your product affects their company's productivity numbers. Finally, your customers' frontline workers are the best source for discovering how your product or service is experienced on a daily basis. They can open your eyes to the ways in which your product is difficult to use, or let you know if your service people are "getting in the way" at times. These small annoyances can provide important clues as to what your company needs to fix, enhance, or eliminate to stay ahead of the competition.

o **A variety of *perspectives*.** Speak with customer employees who are ready for change and those who are averse to it. Also gain the perspective of those who are advocates of your company and those who are advocates of your competitors. In addition, be sure to check in with employees who have different points of view on how their industry is likely to evolve, and different views on opportunities and challenges facing the business.

- **Talk to both satisfied and unsatisfied customers.** Talking to satisfied customers is certainly instructive, because you can find out what they love about you, and strive to do more of that. You can target other customers who have similar needs or who fit a similar profile. Yet it's equally if not more important to talk to unsatisfied customers. Find out what's bothering them, and why. Are they a lost cause—simply a poor fit with your value proposition and capabilities? Or can they provide clues regarding broader market shifts that are critical for your company to respond to?

- **Learn from your hardest-to-please customers.** Your most demanding and advanced customers are those you can learn the most from. For example, Amazon is renowned for pushing its vendors to perform faster, cheaper, and better than before. The e-commerce giant constantly plays hardball with book publishers to extract bigger discounts and, likewise, works assiduously with the delivery services like FedEx, UPS, and the U.S. Postal Service to drive its logistics costs down; Amazon also insists on ever-improving delivery performance.

Amazon has probably been a challenging customer for each of these delivery giants, but they've doubtlessly learned and improved as a result. Although UPS as a matter of policy doesn't talk about individual customers, the company's president of corporate strategy, Ross McCullough, acknowledges that "some of the greatest innovations UPS has developed came as the result of working with customers that were not only demanding but that were also willing to spend time with us collaborating on a problem. When we spend time with customers, we often find latent needs they weren't even aware of. By virtue of the exposure we get from so many other customers, we often see a solution—an innovation—that wasn't apparent to the customer."[4]

When the world's biggest large appliance maker and *Newsweek*'s number-ten most innovative company in the world, Haier, decided to venture beyond its home market of China, it immediately entered America and Europe—rather than beginning in less competitive regions like Southeast Asia and Africa. Haier's CEO Zhang Ruimin wanted the company to learn from serving the world's most challenging and sophisticated consumers.

Because your hardest-to-please customers push their own performance boundaries, they push yours as well. As a result, they are often willing to collaborate with you to improve joint performance—and that's when real breakthroughs happen.

What to Find Out

Once you've figured out what to observe and whom to talk to, then you should determine what it is you want to find out. Here are four things to consider when you're ready to do just that:

- **Find out specifically how your product *creates value* for your customers.** Understand how your customers make money, and what specific impact your product or service has on that process. Do you enable your customers to sell more—and if so, how much more? Do you reduce your customers' costs or the amount of working capital required? Because most customers won't have given much thought to the way your product affects their economics, they aren't likely to have ready answers. Ask for specific examples of when your product or service made a difference to a customer's business results, and help him or her translate this example into a dollar figure. Ask "what-if" questions ("What if we could help you perform this step of your process 20 percent faster? What would that be worth?") Understanding the economics of your customers' business enables you to more intelligently choose where to focus your innovation, and keeps you from wasting time on efforts that don't create value.
- **Help your customers *differentiate*.** Ask your customers why *their* customers choose to buy from them, what their competitive advantage is, and how it might change in the future. Ask about changing market needs and what transformations are occurring in the competitive environment where their companies play. Ask what you can do to further differentiate them in the eyes of their customers.
- **Discern what *motivates* customer employees emotionally and from an "incentives" perspective.** It's easy to think of your customers as Company A and Company B—large entities that make decisions based on logic and numbers. But when it comes to choosing a vendor, *individual people* ultimately make the decision. It's important, then, to know what motivates customer decision makers and how you can

help them meet their personal goals. Understanding what they would like to accomplish, and how your company can help them accomplish it, is essential.

- **Understand your customers'** *entire ecosystem.* Companies often exist to serve a complex network of constituencies (see Figure 4.1). Seek to understand how your customers' customers' needs are changing and how the capabilities and offerings of your customers' other suppliers are changing. Look at your customers' entire ecosystem of partners, advisers, and collaborators. This sounds time consuming, but it doesn't need to be. Sometimes just a couple of additional questions during a customer interview can uncover opportunities to create more value for everyone involved.

All of these tips have their counterpart in the consumer products world. So if you sell to consumers, observe how your product is distributed, presented on the shelf, sold, stored, consumed, and disposed of. Who is involved in or influences each of these stages? Whom can you talk to at each stage of this process to fully understand what changes are occurring and what opportunities might exist?

Enlist the Customer as Collaborator

Airbnb engaged customers in the innovation process by meeting with them in their cities, staying with them as a guest, or hosting them. AGCO went to the farms and spent in-depth time with farmers. Both of these companies implicitly enlisted their customers as collaborators in the innovation process. Customers contributed ideas and insights while also energizing the Airbnb and AGCO teams.

It's far easier to find creative ways around roadblocks if you've got a *specific customer* in mind—an actual person whose problem you can solve. Being married to the problem means being so mentally and emotionally connected to your customer's problem that you go to bed thinking about it and wake up thinking about it. The problem invigorates you. Every stranger you meet and every conversation you have, whether personal or professional, seems to relate to it somehow.

Enlisting the customer as collaborator also enables you to understand—and ultimately communicate—how your product or service contributes to the customer's growth, profits, and purpose. Your customers have a lot of things to think about other than you, so your ability to articulate this contribution is crucial to staying on their mind. When you can express how you help customers succeed—using their language—you will find that they will readily collaborate with you. This collaboration, in turn, enables you to be more agile and adaptive in creating ever-increasing value for the customer.

Know What Problems You Are Trying to Solve

Successfully adapting to changes in your customer's needs requires a deep understanding of the problem you are trying to solve for the customer and how you can help him or her solve that problem.

Harvard Business School professor and author Clay Christensen, Intuit chief executive officer Scott Cook, and Taddy Hall provide a great example in their *Harvard Business Review* article "Marketing Malpractice: The Cause and the Cure." The article examines a fast-food restaurant's effort to improve milkshake sales. The company first took a conventional approach, surveying prospective milkshake buyers to determine what changes they would like in the product's taste, price point, texture, and other measures. However, the implemented changes had no impact on sales.

The restaurant then conducted research into what problems consumers really wished to solve when they purchased a milkshake. It found that a surprising proportion—fully 40 percent—of milkshakes were purchased in the early morning, by solo customers who consumed the shake in their car. The researchers found that customers were trying not only to satisfy their hunger until lunchtime but also to reduce the boredom of their morning commute. Customers didn't want to fool with packaging or to risk spilling crumbs or sauces on their work clothes. A milkshake was thick, so it took a long time to sip on the way to work. They could use one hand while driving with the other, and it was not messy. These consumers were not purchasing the milkshake to be healthy, but it was probably a plus that it didn't "count" as extra calories, as it replaced an equally caloric breakfast food. And perhaps people could feel somewhat good that it contained protein and milk, which they had been taught were healthy for them.

Looking at the milkshake in terms of the problem it solved for the consumer—the job the consumer wanted the shake to do—enabled the company to do two things. First, this approach allowed the company to "de-average" the milkshake-drinking populations, separating out the solo morning commuters from the parents who purchased a shake as part of a meal for their kids, and the teens who purchased it as part of a social outing. Second, through its understanding of why customers were buying the shake, the company was better able to enhance the shake's value for these customers. On the basis of this research, the company invested in making the milkshake an even better cure for the boring morning commute. They made the shake even thicker so that it would last longer, and added bits of fruit to supply an element of unpredictability and anticipation to the morning drive. Illuminating the problem led to a more valuable and differentiated solution.

Understand Your Customers' Hearts, Minds, Habits, and Values

When Hala Moddelmog became president of fast-food chain Arby's in May 2010, she found that the restaurant was "eighteen years behind" in offering a value menu.[5] While McDonald's, Wendy's, Taco Bell, and others were all rolling out new "99 cent" value-meal offerings during the difficult economy of 2008–2010, Arby's held steady on price. As a result, the chain lost 20 to 25 percent of top-line revenue, causing EBITDA to fall from 22 to 25 percent to below 10 percent. Further, Arby's had been losing money for four straight years prior to Moddelmog's arrival.

While financial results at the parent company had declined, the impact on the franchisees was perhaps even more severe. For years, Arby's had fallen further behind the competition, and had a lot of catching up to do. However, Moddelmog didn't want to just catch up; she wanted Arby's to leap *ahead* of competitors. Upon her arrival, Moddelmog made it her goal to deeply understand the Arby's consumer and where her company could most productively invest to grow sales.

In 2011, Arby's began this process by surveying six thousand consumers to learn the basics of how they were dining in the quick-service category. The company discovered that 63 percent of Arby's sales were attributed to only 18 percent of consumers. These consumers were heavy fast-food consumers who dined at quick-service and casual-dining restaurants an astonishing fifty to sixty times per month, and at Arby's six to seven times each month.

Operating on the assumption that it would be harder to attract new consumers than to attract these consumers to the chain more frequently, Arby's set out to discover who they were, what they valued most, and how Arby's could win more of their business. The company figured that if it focused on this core 18 percent and could increase their visits to Arby's by even one time per month, overall sales results would climb by 10 percent or more. It was therefore well worth investing to find out what these consumers wanted and how Arby's could better satisfy them.

Early in 2012, Moddelmog assembled a team that included a videographer and an anthropologist trained in ethnography—that is, research designed to explore cultural phenomena—to visit and spend two to four hours in the homes of about one hundred of these core consumers.[6] Not disclosing that they were from Arby's, the team sought to understand how food figured in these people's lives, how they viewed the world, and what their values were. Some of the families felt nervous at first, but became relaxed as the researchers chatted with them about their values, their family, and what was of interest to them. At some point, the researchers would narrow the discussion to focus on food.

The researchers wanted to deeply understand these consumers and their eating habits. After establishing rapport, they asked if they could visit the kitchen. They opened the cupboards and looked in the refrigerator. They videotaped what they saw. They looked at key chains to see what loyalty programs the consumers belonged to, and noticed what leftovers and sauce packets the family had on hand.

Finally, the researchers asked if they could take the family out to lunch or dinner at the restaurant of their choice. Some chose Arby's. Others chose another brand. The researchers dined with them to better understand how these consumers experienced quick-service dining.

Arby's developed an understanding of that 18 percent of customers who drive 63 percent of the company's sales as "modern-day traditionalists." Although these consumers come from many different age groups, ethnic groups, and types of families, they hold similar values and beliefs.[7] In an article about Arby's revitalization, writer Melissa French characterized the brand's core customers: "They like the truth, without fluff; they have robust patriotism and strong family values; and most importantly, they are interested in whether a product does what it says it's going to do."[8] These consumers lead very busy lives. They are not wealthy, and they need to fit eating into the time that they have between work and taking the kids to school, soccer games, and other activities. The company also found that the modern-day traditionalist is relatively skeptical of novelty and change. "It's a rational, no-nonsense group," explained Arby's chief marketing officer at the time, Russ Klein, ". . . that prefers the familiar with a twist, rather than something they've never heard of or [which] is specifically on trend."[9] Consequently, the company had to be careful not to stray too far from the basics when introducing new products.

The company's quantitative market research also guided its moves. They found, for example, that one of its key differentiators—the fact that meats are sliced fresh right at the store, rather than arriving presliced—wasn't something customers understood or appreciated. Only 56 percent of fast-food customers knew that each Arby's restaurant slices meat in-store daily. Of even more concern was the fact that a similar number—57 percent—believed that Subway, a competitor of Arby's, slices its meat fresh in the store, even though Subway actually slices its meat in a factory.[10] Getting this information out to consumers was essential to differentiating the brand in consumers' minds.

Arby's began to focus every move on these modern-day traditionalists. From product development, to refreshing its iconic "cowboy hat" logo, to sponsoring the No Kid Hungry campaign to end childhood hunger in the United States, to restaurant remodeling—everything revolved around attracting and pleasing this group.

In the end, Arby's in-depth research helped save the brand. As president of Arby's through October 2013, Moddelmog led a remarkable turnaround, driving twelve consecutive quarters of comparable store sales increases.[11]

Understand How Your Customers Vary Across Cultures and Geographies

To serve customers well, it is helpful to understand attitudinal and psychographic segments, and to know which segments are largest and most important and how they vary between geographic markets.

Fortunately, distilling how customers think in a given geographic market does not necessarily mean you have to physically visit that market. Kimberly-Clark's Professional Products group, which sells paper towels, sanitizers, antiviral tissues, and the like to businesses, wanted to change the conversation with its customers. Instead of competing on price, it wanted to solve its customers' higher-order needs, such as health and wellness, employee productivity, and sustainability.

When people come to work sick, they aren't at the top of their game; they may even be "under the influence" of cold medicines that further dull their performance. In a production environment where an employee mistake can even endanger other workers, being in top form at work is critical.

Kimberly-Clark wanted to help its customers worldwide to improve their employees' health and wellness. The company believed that behavior change—to reduce transmission of germs at work—was a key lever. But in order to incite this change, it first needed to understand people's general attitudes about germs. So it hosted online focus groups in fifteen different countries, from Russia to India and beyond. Because the focus groups were held over a two-week period, the discussion had time to percolate, and participants could build on each other's ideas. The online focus groups also allowed the company to attract a high-quality, diverse group of people, because participants did not all have to be available to travel to a focus-group site at the same time of day. They could check in and respond multiple times a day and at odd hours.

The company distilled country-to-country differences in how people viewed germs and the spread of disease. It found that people in Russia did not feel comfortable talking with others about germs or about the chance of passing a cold, flu, or other contagious disease to others, whereas such talk was acceptable in the

United States, even in workplace settings. In India, most people traveled to work on crowded, dirty public transportation systems, so their greatest concern was being clean and professional when they reported to work. Brazil was one of the most germ-conscious markets; in that country, even floors are washed daily with bleach.

This research, along with interviews with consumers, managers, educators, and experts throughout the world, formed the basis of a deep understanding of how individuals think about germs and contagious disease in the workplace, and how the spread of disease could be reduced through behavior change. The company made a point of talking to people at the fringe, such as those who self-identified as germophobes. Researchers swabbed germ "hotspots" like phones, break room refrigerators, and elevator buttons to understand where germs lurked. They met with general managers, human resource leaders, and industrial managers who stood to benefit from the programs Kimberly-Clark envisioned, showing them video storyboards demonstrating how employee behaviors could be changed.

The company used its research results to create the Healthy Workplace Project, a set of products, services, games, and communication tools to improve wellness. They implemented the program in fifty countries over three years—and found it to have profound effects on workplace wellness. Although it often took from 90 to 120 days to effect behavior change, germ counts declined dramatically once that was done. The company estimates that organizations which implement the Healthy Workplace Project can save on the order of $20 per employee per month due to decreased absenteeism and reduced medical and pharmacy claims expenses. The program also generated another, very surprising, outcome: employee engagement scores at participating companies improved by 20 to 30 points.

Without its deep investment in understanding global views on germs, Kimberly-Clark would not have been able to leap ahead of competitors. It would not have been able to shift the conversation with business customers from just talking about price to working together to improve employee wellness, productivity, and engagement.

In Conclusion

By digging deeply into your customers' problems and needs, you are likely to find new insights that will help you gain an edge against your competitors. You can achieve these insights by doing the following:

- **Focus on the problem you are trying to solve for your customer.** It's easy to waste time and money chasing innovations, initiatives, and product improvement ideas that your customer does not value. First, determine what problems your customers want solved—and then focus on solving them.
- **Understand not just purchasers of your product or service but the full spectrum of people who use it.** If you are in a business-to-business market, talk to and observe a range of people within your customers' organizations—not just those responsible for the buying decision. Look even more broadly at each customer's entire ecosystem, to notice changes and opportunities.
- **Enlist the customer as collaborator.** By doing so, you find out directly the problems they need solved and the solutions they prefer. When AGCO wanted to understand its customers' needs better, the company spent significant time with farmers *on* their farms, observing in depth what equipment they used to do their work and how they used it.
- **Immerse yourself in key customers' lives.** Arby's teams visited target customers for several hours in their homes, looking in their refrigerators, eating with them, and probing to understand their values. They developed a deep understanding of their customers' needs, which allowed them to successfully innovate and adapt.

- **Understand how your customers vary across cultures and geographies.** Focus groups, online surveys, and other approaches can help you understand how customers think in different geographic markets. Understanding these differences will allow you to tailor the approaches you use—marketing messages, packaging, even the products themselves—to specific audiences.

Chapter Five

Turn Trends into Opportunities

Stop Preparing for the Future and Create It

On Cyber Monday 2013, one of the busiest small-package shipping days of the year, I visited UPS's Worldport air hub in Louisville, Kentucky. Beginning at about 11:30 p.m. on December 2, more than 130 cargo aircraft began descending from all around the world—one every sixteen to ninety seconds. UPS workers unloaded the packages, set them label side up on the conveyor belt, and sent them on an automated journey through a maze of conveyers so fast and convoluted that watching them was literally dizzying. Thirteen-and-a-half minutes later, after having been touched by human hands exactly twice, each package was miraculously spit out at the exact spot where an aircraft was waiting to take it on the next leg of its journey. By 2:50 a.m., the aircraft—chock-full of packages and recharged with fuel and flight crews—began departing from Worldport to make the early morning delivery schedule.

What I witnessed that day—a complex, highly automated sorting facility the size of ninety football fields—will continue to evolve in the coming years. From its beginnings, UPS has adapted quickly and effectively to the changes it sees in the market. When the company was launched in 1907, it focused on delivering messages by foot and bicycle. Within a few years, however, the spread of telephones ended the need for message carriers. The company shifted its focus to package delivery, persuading grocery, drug, and department stores to outsource their delivery services, and stationing UPS employees on-site at the stores to manage distribution.

After World War II, as automobiles became commonplace and suburban malls with large parking lots sprang up, stores no longer needed to deliver to consumers. So UPS adapted once again, shifting the focus to delivering packages to business and private addresses, and becoming the first package delivery company to serve the forty-eight contiguous states.

Threats to UPS have come not only from changes in culture, the economy, and customer needs but also from competition. In 1971, a student at Yale, Fred Smith, wrote a paper proposing a new concept: an overnight delivery service in which all packages would be flown by aircraft to a central clearinghouse each night, where they could be sorted and dispatched, arriving at their destination the next day.

Smith's company, Federal Express, was officially launched in 1973, revolutionizing package delivery and presenting an entirely new type of competition for UPS. With its compelling offering of "when it absolutely, positively has to be there overnight" and its sophisticated computer systems to manage people, packages, vehicles, and weather in real time, FedEx grew fast. In 1983, it became the first company in American history to reach $1 billion in revenue in less than ten years without a merger.[1]

Again, UPS coped effectively with change. By 1985, it had assembled its own fleet of aircraft, and UPS Next Day Air service was available in all fifty states.

Today, UPS is in an enviable position. The company reaches more recipients globally than any other player in the parcel shipment business, earning the highest operating margins in its industry—13 percent—versus only 9 percent for FedEx and DHL.[2] It moves an average of sixteen million packages daily and is an exceptionally operationally efficient company, filled with smart industrial engineering, logistics, and information technology experts. Still, the company is not immune to threats. It must remain vigilant in identifying—and agile in responding to—changes in the marketplace.

How Can We Best Assess and Respond to Market Change?

How can we deal more effectively with the trends that affect our businesses—and even use these trends to our advantage? In both our business and personal lives, we use a very simple process for surveying our environment and deciding the best course of action; we use it many times per day, when driving to work, answering an email, or cooking dinner. Figure 5.1 illustrates this process:

The first step in the process is simply **to notice what is going on around you**—to see the risks, trends, and potential changes that might affect you.

The second step is to **decide which changes matter**—which represent significant opportunities or threats. Prioritizing at this stage is important; if you respond to every change you see, you'll spread your resources too thin and won't get anything done very effectively. You are likely to confuse your employees and customers and risk wasting resources responding to changes that will have little impact on your business success.

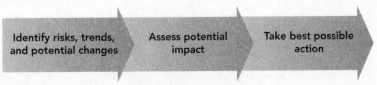

Figure 5.1 Identifying Change and Taking Action

The third step is to **decide how you are going to respond**. Subsequent chapters will bring to light techniques for identifying the alternatives for dealing with each important change you see in your business environment and determining the best possible course of action.

What Types of Market Change Do We Need to Be Concerned About?

Let's look at the challenges and opportunities that UPS faces today. The company monitors many trends in its business environment—current and potential changes in buying preferences, environmental regulations, competitive offerings, the flow of goods between countries, and much more. UPS then must decide where to place its resources to respond effectively.

Here are just a few of the market changes to which UPS must respond:

Pressure on margins
- As e-commerce grows, the portion of package volume that comprises lower-margin, business-to-consumer shipments compared to higher-margin, business-to-business shipments has grown.
- Online retailers are increasingly offering free shipping, especially around the busiest holiday periods. Because retailers are subsidizing the shipping costs, this increases the retailers' resolve to negotiate hard with parcel delivery companies on price.
- In an attempt to offset revenue losses in its highest-margin first-class mail business, the United States Postal Service (USPS) is aggressively marketing its Priority Mail services at prices that are hard for UPS to match and still turn a profit. Further, the USPS has vastly improved its package tracking, making its service more compelling for shippers.[3]

Pressure on revenue

- Amazon is building "fulfillment centers" or distribution warehouses closer to its customers and using its own delivery trucks. It has also become more sophisticated at combining multiple orders into the same box, further reducing package volume. As Amazon reduces its shipping costs and brings more shipping activities in-house, it lessens its reliance on UPS and the other package delivery services.
- Major brick-and-mortar retailers such as Walmart, Best Buy, and The Gap are shipping more online orders from stores that are close to shoppers, rather than shipping from warehouses hundreds of miles away. This reduces the distance that parcel delivery companies carry the packages, and likewise reduces shipping revenues.

International opportunities

- Although e-commerce shipping volumes are growing fast in the United States, they are rising much faster in the rest of the world, outside UPS's home market. The growth of the middle class in many developing countries as well as the surge in international trade is behind this trend. Further, some major companies have found it advantageous to locate inventory in places like China, where labor costs for packing and shipping orders are low.

Macroeconomic changes

- Relatively high interest rates in the 1980s and 1990s enticed companies to consolidate inventory into just a few distribution centers, so that inventory could be held to the minimum. The extremely low interest rates between 2008 and 2014, however, presented a very different cost equation, prompting the pendulum to swing the other way. Storing inventory at multiple points close to customers is no longer as expensive as it used to be. Holding inventory close to customers, of course, translates to shorter shipping distances and less revenue for the package delivery companies.

- Fuel prices—and therefore, fuel surcharges—have risen significantly in the past decade. In response, UPS customers have opted for cheaper delivery options. Packages that would have formerly traveled via a premium overnight service now may travel by the much lower-priced "ground" option—a "trading down" tendency that negatively affects UPS revenues.

Reshoring

- North American companies that offshored manufacturing ten or twenty years ago to take advantage of lower labor costs in Asia have seen Chinese wages rise fivefold since 2000. Meanwhile, advances in automation technology mean that they need far fewer workers for some jobs. Some companies are beginning to reshore—that is, move manufacturing operations *to* the United States and Mexico, where they can enjoy reasonable costs, flexible workforces, and more nimble innovation cycles. Although the shift may be limited in scope, this is a modestly favorable trend for UPS, with its home base in North America and its historical focus on the manufacturing industry.

New technologies

- Numerous technologies—from hands-free computing like Google Glass, drone-based delivery systems, and voice recognition to miniaturization and 3D printing—have the potential to transform UPS's operations and markets. For example, dental implants, which historically have been shipped via package delivery services, will now be able to be made right in the dentist's office using 3D printers.

Regulatory changes

- Governments in the United States, Europe, and elsewhere may tighten legislation to reduce the carbon emissions of logistics firms and others, while new technologies for powering vehicles are being developed at a rapid pace.

Later in this chapter, we'll look at some of the actions UPS is taking to respond to these trends. For now, let's look at how you can identify the forces that may affect *your* business—and take appropriate action.

How Can We Best Identify and Prioritize the Marketplace Changes That May Affect Our Business?

Company leaders often feel buffeted by changes in competitor capability and strategy, customer demand, and economic conditions. These executives see new technologies, but aren't sure when to invest so that their technology will not become obsolete. Kodak, for example, famously invented the digital camera in 1975, but then watched from the sidelines as other companies—beginning with Sony and its Mavica camera in 1981—grew digital photography into a huge market, and made Kodak and its film cameras (and paper and chemicals) largely obsolete.[4]

Companies *know* they should make bold, strategic moves. However, they worry about the risks and uncertainties involved in taking such leaps. You never know how slippery or unstable the next rock might be when jumping from stone to stone to cross a river. Hop to the wrong rock, and you'll end up with boots full of water; slip, and you might drown.

Dealing effectively with change—be it to capitalize on opportunities or to mitigate potential threats—starts with anticipating what is *likely to happen*. Figure 5.2 provides a thought-starter for

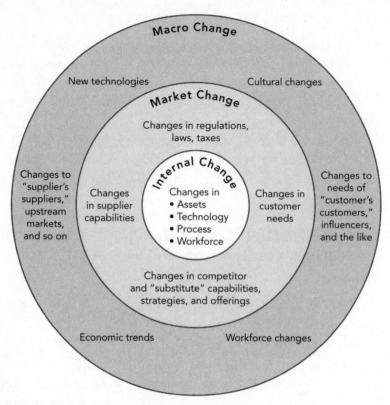

Figure 5.2 Changes in Your Business, Your Markets, and the World

identifying the changes that may occur in your business, your markets, and the world as a whole.

Macro changes, in the outer band of Figure 5.2, include such things as demographic trends, the emergence of new technologies, economic and cultural trends, and the like. Examples include the aging population, new concerns about obesity and sustainability, and consumers' growing reliance on social media for recommendations on what to buy.

Teasing out the *real* impact these macro trends have on your business can be difficult—and might even seem like a theoretical or futile exercise. After all, you might wonder why, if you supply parts for paper machines, you should care about issues like social media, obesity, and demographic shifts.

Here's where imagination comes in. What might the *effects* of these trends be? Will—or could—any have an impact on the consumption of packaged foods, or the sizes of the paper containers that are used? Will they affect the amount of printed material that people use, the number of office workers, the number of telecommuters, or the resulting use of office papers? To understand how each macro trend might affect your business, ask yourself: How might this trend affect

- What our customers want?
- Our company's current and potential capability relative to the customer's alternatives?
- Our suppliers, our customers' customers, and others in our business ecosystem?

Market changes, shown in the middle band of Figure 5.2, include changes that directly affect your company, though they may or may not be easy to see. Chapters 2, 3, and 4 offered guidance on how to identify these changes, which include the emergence of new supplier capabilities, the merger of two competitors, new regulations governing your industry, or changes in the way customers buy or use your products—and your competitors'.

Internal changes include events, trends, and changes inside your company that could have a lasting and strategic impact or that will consume a large share of management attention and resources. Examples include the addition of new production capacity, the implementation of a new technology, changes in your workforce, or the introduction of a new process for managing orders or customer service.

Anticipate What Might Happen Next

After you identify the changes that you see in your macro environment, your market, and within your company, you should think about what might happen next—and what the impact might be. Unfortunately, too many people skip this valuable exercise. In some instances, they see a threat and hope it will go away (the "head in the sand" syndrome). In others, they assume that they know the outcome and implement the most obvious course of action—such as cutting prices to match the competition instead of finding ways to increase value to customers. Trouble is, the "obvious" action is often dead wrong. Even if it's a logical response, it's often the *same* response your competitor chooses—leaving you in the predicament of being in an undifferentiated competitive position.

You should also assess the degree of uncertainty associated with each change. If a change is highly certain—that is, if you know exactly what will happen, when it will happen, how it will happen, and how it will affect your business—the proper response is usually straightforward. You assign resources, approve the budget, and move forward. Although it's not always that simple, well-understood changes are usually the ones that companies are best prepared to deal with.

Table 5.1 presents an example of how one company assessed the changes it confronted. The changes are listed in the first column—"macro" at the top, "market" in the middle, and the most "internal" toward the bottom of the table. Thinking of it this way—from the *outside in*—enabled the team to view their situation most broadly at the beginning of the exercise before tackling any internal issues. This prevents internal changes—usually, the ones we deal with daily—from dominating the conversation and share of mind.

It is usually best to assign the exercise shown in Table 5.1 as a solo pursuit before discussing it as a group. Different employees have different views of the changes that are occurring, given the variations in their own, their spouse's, friends', and relatives' occupations, the publications they read—even the diverse views of the customers, suppliers, and other stakeholders with whom

Table 5.1 Anticipating What Might Happen, and Assessing Impact and Uncertainty (Example)

Area of Change (Listed in order from "most macro" to "most internal")	What Evidence Do We See?	What Might Happen?	Impact	Uncertainty
A growing number of customers want to use mobile technologies to research products and transact.	Orders placed via smartphone or tablet have increased 20% this year (but are still only 8% of sales); 100 customers per month use our mobile app without transacting.	We are likely to lose sales if we don't improve our mobile app; if we develop a great app, we could build substantial loyalty and differentiation.	H	H
It's increasingly difficult to find employees with the skills we need.	Five positions in engineering and two in inside sales have gone unfilled for more than six months.	More than half of our sales require some engineering involvement to close. Filling these roles is crucial.	M	L
New regulations may require package redesign.	Regulators are considering new rules, which may render current packaging inadequate.	If redesign is required, it will be complex—and may take 6–12 months. If we are not prepared, we could lose sales or increase development costs. If we do it well, we could gain share while other competitors are distracted.	L	L
More customers require shorter lead times, and rush orders are increasing.	Customers asked for less than 48-hour delivery on 20% of orders in Northeast region and 30% in Midwest (up from 5% and 12% last year).	This new customer requirement gives us an opportunity to stand out from competitors. However, we will lose sales if we do not add swing capacity or increase inventory levels.	M	M
A competitor is rumored to be developing an ultra-low-cost product line.	Two customers mentioned this to our salespeople in the last three months.	If this new product meets customer needs, it could hurt sales. But could we reinforce our "premium" positioning if the competitor goes down-market?	H	H

(Continued)

Table 5.1 Anticipating What Might Happen, and Assessing Impact and Uncertainty (Example) (*Continued*)

Area of Change (Listed in order from "most macro" to "most internal")	What Evidence Do We See?	What Might Happen?	Impact	Uncertainty
A supplier is introducing higher-performance materials, but the cost will likely be 20% higher.	The supplier's R&D manager mentioned this to us last month (the product is not expected for 1–2 more years).	We have an opportunity to introduce a premium product, if customer demand is there.	L	H
Key salespeople are retiring.	Fifteen salespeople are retiring in the next 18 months; 10% of the sales force is likely to retire in next 3 years.	We risk losing sales if we don't transition our accounts effectively. At the same time, these retirements give us an opportunity to bring in fresh talent and to reduce selling cost.	H	L
Implementation of the new ERP system may disrupt business.	U.S. implementation will be complete in December and in Europe next year.	We will be short-handed in finance until implementation is complete, and may experience hiccups in the order-fulfillment process. However, the ERP will give us new capabilities to manage rush orders and cater to special customer needs.	L	L

they work. In addition, some people are far more creative and thoughtful when they have time to think without outside influence. Give individuals a week to fill out the table, come together to assemble the responses, and then discuss them as a group to discern: What have we left out? Do we have consensus on the potential impact and uncertainty of each change? If not, why not?

After agreeing on a first draft of the table, let it sit for a week or two. Encourage individuals on the team to consider the changes that populated the first column and to talk to others about them—both within and outside your company. Allow them time to research and think about the ideas that they did not put forward during their solo exercise but that a colleague contributed.

This exercise provides you with an opportunity to learn from the unexpected. Too often, companies see only what they *expect to see* and fail to notice aberrations. Unanticipated successes, failures, or market events are often a sign that something is changing in your business environment. When you or your colleagues notice something unexpected, explore it. Why did this occur now and *not* before? What does this say about how things are changing?

After giving your team a week or two to review the results of the first draft of this table, you can gather again and revise your list. When you have consensus, move to the next step.

Prioritize and Take Action

The next step is to graph these opportunities and threats, with potential impact on the y-axis, and uncertainty—or the degree to which you can predict what will happen, when it will happen, and how it will affect your business—on the x-axis. Figure 5.3 shows how this would look for the example in Table 5.1.

The top right quadrant of Figure 5.3, labeled "Assess strategic alternatives and then respond" is where the high-impact, high-uncertainty changes lie. These are your highest strategic

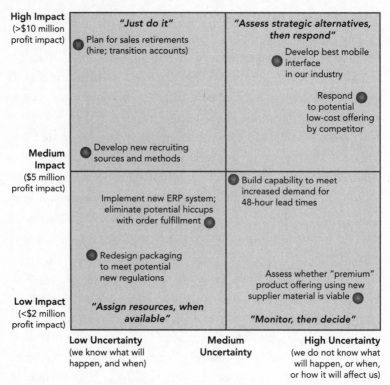

Figure 5.3 Prioritizing Our Response to Changes

priorities—those opportunities and threats that your best thinkers and leaders should focus on to answer the following questions:

- What are the **possible outcomes** of the trend or change? What is the **likelihood** of each?
- Which **strategic alternatives** should we consider for **each possible outcome**? What initiatives, investments, or actions would maximize the potential positive impact—and minimize the potential negative impact?
- What should we do to **measure or monitor** the potential change? For example, should we have additional conversations with customers or perform market research? Should we enlist the help of outside experts to advise us on the best way to proceed?

The important thing to remember about the top right box is that even very troubling trends can create opportunities. For example—when Arm & Hammer baking soda maker Church and Dwight noticed that people were baking less at home, the company successfully expanded into deodorant, toothpaste, pet care, vacuum bags, and other products. If Church and Dwight leaders had not noticed what they considered at the time to be a worrying trend, the company may never have discovered the many lucrative, high-growth product opportunities it later exploited. Consumers now associate Church and Dwight's Arm & Hammer brand with fresh fragrance, wholesome goodness, and cleanliness across a wide range of applications—not just baking soda.

The top left quadrant of the figure is labeled "Just do it"—because these changes are high impact and low uncertainty. Here, you understand the nature of the changes that are coming, and you know how to deal with them. Your company should take action immediately to maximize the positive impact and minimize the negative in these cases.

The bottom left quadrant is labeled "Assign resources, when available." Although these changes are certainly coming, their impact is low. If you are short of resources, as most companies are, you can afford to wait until after you have dealt with the higher-impact changes.

Finally, the bottom right quadrant is labeled "Monitor, then decide." These include highly uncertain changes. You don't know when they will occur, the extent to which they will occur—or even if they will occur at all. The best course of action in these cases is to determine what measures, market indicators, or events you should keep an eye on to give you more information about the potential change.

One secret to monitoring highly uncertain potential changes is to identify "triggers" that alert you to meaningful changes in the trends most relevant to your business. For example, you might look for an uptick in sales of a particular product, or flag an increase in certain types of customer complaints, comments, or requests. Industry associations or market measurement services can often provide data on market share, competitor capacity utilization, and total production for the industry. Stock prices, commodity price data, and government data, such as U.S. Department of Commerce trade figures, give good benchmarks for both an industry's health and the outlook for demand. There is an amazing amount of data available for those who look for it. Just ask yourself, "What would I love to know?"—and then take a look. It's often surprising how much information a quick Google search can turn up.

Once these triggers have alerted you, you can decide how to respond to the opportunity or threat. Sure, it would be nice to decide right away. But remember that all of your best resources, time, and money are devoted to opportunities and threats that are located in the top two boxes of your graph.

Companies that become fixated on watching trends have managers that are distracted from their crucial daily priorities. Other companies are lulled to sleep by the slow pace at which some trends materialize and are caught unprepared when the trend begins to harm their performance.

What Action Is UPS Taking to Respond to the Changes in Its Business Environment?

As we discussed earlier in this chapter, UPS is not sitting idly on the sidelines as change roils its industry. Instead, the company is actively seeking new opportunities while addressing potential competitive threats and challenges. The following are some specific actions that UPS is taking.

Investment in Customer Collaboration

UPS believes that it must develop truly differentiated solutions to maintain its industry-leading margins, so it has trained its sales and field-marketing staff to help customers identify pain points and opportunities within their supply chains—and then develop the strategies that enable these customers to achieve their business goals.

An example is UPS Returns Exchange, in which UPS delivers a replacement item as it simultaneously collects the return shipment. For example—if a consumer has a problem with a tablet she has purchased, the UPS driver can pick up, package, and ship the defective unit and deliver a replacement during the same visit. The defective unit can be routed directly back to a repair center, destruction facility, or manufacturer, which often eliminates a leg in the shipping journey. The system makes for a better customer experience and reduces fraud risk, shipping costs, and the cycle time for returns.

Imagine the other ways that customers could utilize UPS Returns Exchange. What if a UPS driver could, on a regular schedule, pick up an empty oxygen tank from the home of a pulmonary patient and simultaneously deliver a new one? Or bring important legal forms, wait for the recipient to sign them, then repackage them and send them on their way? UPS has equipped its sales and marketing staff to discover and solve unique customer problems such as these.

Emulate UPS's example in your own organization by **learning from your customers** and **innovating to serve their needs**.

Providing Expert Logistics Advice and Outsourced Supply Chain Management

As brick-and-mortar retailers seek ways to compete with Amazon and other e-commerce companies, being able to ship directly to consumers from inventory held in the store is key to reducing shipping costs and shortening delivery times. But although the store workforce is expert at merchandising and sales, it isn't well versed in picking, packaging, and shipping product. UPS consults with these retailers to understand the typical store layout, the range of stores that exist, and the type of personnel the retailer employs. UPS then works with the retailer to build a master operating plan for doing store-based distribution, including reconfiguring the store's back room to accommodate high-volume shipping. This strategy can shave days off shipping time, and dollars off shipping cost.

Enabling ship-from-store and omnichannel retailing is one way UPS helps its customers adapt to changing market conditions. The company also helps manage the supply chain for customers such as consumer electronics companies—not only by fulfilling tens of thousands of direct-to-consumer e-commerce orders per day but also by replenishing stock in stores and accepting customer returns. UPS will even load custom software and contact lists onto phones.

You can emulate UPS's example in your own organization by **leveraging your expertise and distinctive capabilities to help your customers adjust to changing competitive conditions in the markets they serve.**

Expansion in the Health Care Logistics Arena

As UPS has attempted to maintain its margins in the face of price pressure in its core markets, the company has sought out opportunities to serve customers with specialized needs that are critical and often time- and temperature-sensitive—thereby allowing UPS to better differentiate its service. The health care market is a great example. The demanding needs of health care customers, combined with the high value of the products being shipped, present an attractive opportunity. Health care providers like Medtronic and ConvaTec outsource their logistics so that they can focus on their core business of developing and rolling out new products. UPS employs full-time pharmacists at its health care campus in Louisville, Kentucky, to process Medtronic direct-to-patient orders, and coordinates a wide range of ConvaTec's supply chain functions in the United

States and Europe—including order entry, warehousing, ship-ping, call-center services, and accounts receivable. As a result, ConvaTec is able to ship orders as late as 10 p.m. for next-day delivery—something that would not have been possible previously. ConvaTec also has improved collections to the point that "days sales outstanding" has been reduced by 30 percent.

UPS built many new capabilities when it entered the health care logistics business, including providing ironclad security for handling controlled and theft-prone prescription drugs. The company added −80 degrees Celsius (−112 degrees Fahrenheit) freezers to store Shire Regenerative Medicine's skin graft product, Dermagraft. The grafts are packaged in specially insulated boxes with dry ice and shipped daily to doctors to treat diabetic foot ulcers.

When a large, global pharmaceutical company based in India needed a way to be first to market with the launch of generic products, it turned to UPS. Despite knowing when its competitors' patents were due to expire, the company couldn't always predict when the Food and Drug Administration (FDA) would approve its generics. Further, the FDA sometimes demanded last-minute changes to the product information labels, which provide drug information to patients. Getting new generics on the shelves of chain drugstores and mass merchandisers within a day of FDA approval can create a huge and lasting market-share advantage, so the company chose to stage product at the UPS health care facility in anticipation of FDA approval. It found that with as little as two hours notice, UPS could assemble three hundred people for a product launch, including printing and replacing product information labels. By partnering with UPS, the pharmaceutical company was able to improve speed to market, in several cases being first on the shelves when FDA approval was gained.

UPS now has six million square feet of warehouse space in forty dedicated health care logistics facilities, in the Americas, Europe, Asia, and Australia. Although it has had to add many new capabilities to serve the health care market, health care has proven to be a profitable, high-growth opportunity that offers great value to its customers.

Emulate UPS's example in your own organization by **seeking out more demanding market segments and customers**. These often offer great potential for customer loyalty and high margins.

Experimentation and Learning in "Green" Technologies

UPS believes that it must be prepared for any new environmental, emissions, and fuel-related regulations that policymakers might impose. In fact, preparing now—*before* regulations are imposed—may enable UPS to create a substantial competitive advantage over companies that wait until they are forced to make changes in their fleets.

To this end, the company invested more than $250 million between 2007 and 2013 in testing different types of vehicles and in developing the operating procedures to optimize their performance.[5] UPS's fleet includes vehicles with bodies made of lightweight composites, and a wide variety of alternative-fuel vehicles, including compressed natural gas, hybrid electric, liquid natural gas, electric, hydraulic hybrid, and propane vehicles. Although these represent only 3 percent (3,142) of UPS's 103,000 vehicles, they form a critical learning laboratory. Further, as the company invests in these vehicles, its fleet becomes greener. Every new tractor purchased for U.S. operations in 2014 will run on natural gas—a relatively low-emissions, domestically produced, and cost-effective fuel.

Learning how to best match the fuel and technology to the specific needs of each route and situation is critical, so UPS is getting an early start by investing in this process now, before the law requires them to. There are wide variations in the mileage and number of stops among UPS's fleet of package cars, the company's name for the ubiquitous brown trucks we see in our neighborhoods. "In Manhattan, a package car might travel 3 miles in a day; but in Death Valley, it might travel 300," says UPS chief operating officer David Abney. "With such different needs, there is no silver bullet—so we've got to do a lot of testing... Progress requires [that we collaborate] with manufacturers, researchers, nonprofits and governments."[6]

The company also has worked with governments to help shape tax policy and regulations. For example, a gallon of liquid natural gas is taxed the same as a gallon of gasoline in the United States. But because of its lower energy density, it takes 1.7 gallons of LNG to equal the energy output of a gallon of diesel. In examples like these, UPS is working to shift tax policy to be more alternative-fuel-friendly, which will have beneficial effects for the global environment.

Emulate UPS's example in your own organization by **starting to learn early** when new regulations are likely. This will give you an opportunity to meet the coming regulations in a smarter and more efficient way once they are imposed—and keep you steps ahead of your competitors.

International Expansion

UPS must continue to grow its international network to efficiently provide the services its customers demand. International segment revenue at UPS grew from 14 percent of total revenue and 6 percent of operating profit in 2000 to 23 percent of revenue and 25 percent of profit in 2013. The company needs to continue to grow globally to keep pace with shipment trends in the market in general. UPS must surmount complex legal hurdles when entering many of these markets, where monopoly mail services are protected from competition.

We hosted an exchange student from France a couple of summers ago. I was amazed to see that her suitcase contained the exact same clothing brands—Hollister and Abercrombie & Fitch—that kids in our neighborhood were wearing at the time. Since then, teen tastes have shifted toward thrift-store shopping and independent (or at least independent-*looking*) brands. As international shipping costs have become more competitive, I've noticed that consumers, especially younger ones, are as likely to choose something from a thrift store or a one-of-a-kind boutique on another continent as to drive to a store a few miles away.

Emulate UPS's example in your own organization by **investing continuously to build the capability you need when there is a long-term trend** in your industry, like a shift to more international demand.

Cost Reduction

With ever-present pressure from large customers to reduce prices, UPS must work unremittingly to improve efficiency. FedEx is a large, efficient, and formidable competitor; the USPS has the advantage that it drives down almost every street in the United States, six days a week. There's little additional cost involved in adding a package to the USPS mail truck.

To compete effectively in this environment, UPS has added numerous services and technologies to optimize routes and package placement on the vehicles and to enable tracking, logistics cost management, and much more. At the same time, they've expanded the number of delivery options available to customers, adding to the complexity of sorting and routing the packages. Yet they've still managed to reduce costs annually.

UPS uses telematics to monitor thousands of data points on each truck. As a result, it has fine-tuned procedures to the point that drivers often don't need to move more than thirty inches to select the next package off the truck. In recent years, both UPS and FedEx have improved ground transit times by a day for hundreds of ZIP code pairings. For example, a ground shipment from Baltimore to New York City will arrive the next day, at a far lower cost than an air express shipment.[7] Continuous cost reduction is a core part of the UPS culture and operating discipline.

Emulate UPS's example in your own organization by **looking continuously for efficiency improvement opportunities** and finding ways to take out cost without reducing customer value. No company or industry is immune to downward price pressure.

New Services That Cater to the Consumer

As business-to-consumer e-commerce shipments have grown as a percentage of UPS's total business, the company has shifted its focus from catering mainly to the shipper, to offering services targeted at the *receiver*. This is a mindset change for UPS managers, who have historically concentrated on pleasing the person sending the package. If consumers preferentially choose UPS as a parcel delivery service, the hope is that the company can earn greater market share—and perhaps even a price premium. To this end, UPS rolled out "UPS My Choice" in 2011—a service that notifies consumers of pending deliveries and enables them to reroute packages (say, to deliver to their office instead of their home) and pay for premium privileges like having packages delivered within a two-hour window. The jury is out on whether this service—and FedEx's match called Delivery Manager—has engendered brand preference in consumers' minds. However, the services do reduce the carriers' need to make costly multiple attempts at delivery.

Emulate UPS's example in your own organization by not simply catering to your most obvious customer—the one who pays the bills (in UPS's case, the shipper)—but also by **considering how you can please your customers' customers and other entities** within your business ecosystem.

UPS had revenues of $54 billion in 2012. It is a large company known more for operational efficiency than agility. However, each of these examples illustrates how even a hundred-year-old company can—and truly *must*—be adept at looking outside itself to see, anticipate, and respond to market changes. UPS gets ahead of the trends, observing and adapting while setting the standard for others to follow. No company can afford to be complacent in the face of the constant, whitewater change in the business environment and markets. Today's most successful companies all make a habit of avoiding complacency and constantly challenging conventional business "wisdom."

In Conclusion

Rather than prepare for a future that may not arrive in the form or at the time you expect, it's far better to shape the future yourself—which you can do in the following ways:

- **Identify the marketplace changes that may affect your business.** Dealing effectively with change starts by anticipating what is likely to happen. Identify the changes that may occur in your business, markets, and the world.
- **Assess each change's potential impact and degree of uncertainty.** Once you have determined potential coming changes, assess how large each one's impact might be and the degree of uncertainty.
- **Prioritize marketplace changes and take action.** For high-impact and very uncertain changes, take the time to generate a range of alternative approaches—and choose carefully before taking action.
- **Monitor a few metrics that signal impending change.** Single out those metrics that can best alert you to changes in market conditions.
- **Turn even troubling trends into opportunities.** For example, Church and Dwight saw that people were baking less at home, and successfully expanded into deodorant, toothpaste, pet care, vacuum bags, and other products.

Chapter Six

Create Breakthrough Strategies

Generate Creative Alternatives for Capitalizing on the Changes You See

The first prototype of Google's wearable computing technology Google Glass did not make it look very useful. The huge glasses obscured the wearer's face, and numerous wires led to a backpack filled with the heavy batteries required to power the device. Even once the sleek, elegantly designed commercial version was introduced to developers, the product did not strike most people as something they would be able to put to good use. It seemed like a novelty.

Now, however, truly useful, even lifesaving examples of where the Google Glass technology will likely be employed abound. With its hands-free operation, its ability to project information in the user's field of view, and its capacity to let someone else see what the user is seeing, the wearable computer will probably be indispensable in many occupations before long.

Firefighters will be able to view blueprints of a building so that they can navigate more quickly to the source of a fire or to spots where people could be trapped. Aircraft engine maintenance technicians will be able to refer to manuals without having to set down their tools. Physicians will be able to refer to patient records, X-rays, and images while performing surgery, and specialists will be able to coach doctors in rural locations through unfamiliar procedures. Chefs and home cooks alike will be able to read recipes while handling cookware and while measuring and mixing ingredients.

Think of any situation in which your hands are busy, dirty, sterile, full of tools, or otherwise occupied—or any situation in which it would be helpful to have others able to see from your viewpoint—and you can think of an application for Google Glass.

Google's definition of innovation is something that's new, surprising, and radically useful. The company's philosophy is that if it can dream up innovations that are ten times bigger than what exists in the market, it will not only capture more customer demand but also be able to attract more creative talent. Breakthrough ideas such as those that Google constantly seeks are essential fuel for an organization's agility, and the ability to generate them can determine which companies thrive and which ones don't.

So, how can *you* develop truly breakthrough innovations? In this chapter, I explore this question in detail, providing a proven framework for action.

Why Breakthrough Ideas Are Important

No industry is immune to change. The players that devise a different and better way of capitalizing on that change are the ones who emerge as winners. If you respond in the same way as your competitor, you run the risk of becoming—or continuing to be—undifferentiated and commoditized.

Therefore, when you see changes in your industry—whether driven by technology, regulations, evolving customer needs, or some other factor—you must devise a breakthrough strategy for adapting to change. This means developing something that no one else has before, which requires you to apply imagination and creativity.

We talked in the previous chapter about how to identify the trends and market changes affecting your business, and how to prioritize these according to their impact and uncertainty. This chapter will provide direction on how to develop creative and effective alternatives for capitalizing on these potentially high-impact changes.

Even if your business environment is not in as much turmoil as some of today's most volatile industries, you're likely experiencing and observing at least some changes which demand that you rethink the way you do business. And you can rest assured that your competitors have probably noticed some of the same changes and market trends you've observed. You may not be able to come up with something as groundbreaking as Google Glass, but if you simply follow the competitive pack, you'll find yourself stuck in a commodity rut—one that's difficult to get out of. Devising a differentiated—or better yet, a truly breakthrough—strategy is the far better route.

Lessons from AGCO on Developing Breakthrough Strategies

Chapter 4 told the story of AGCO, one of the world's largest agricultural equipment manufacturers. You'll recall that AGCO observed farmers around the world to understand their changing needs and then used these observations to add innovative new technologies to its products. The company shifted from selling only heavy equipment toward selling services, advice, and optimization. The new strategy has paid off in higher margins and sales growth for both the company and its dealers, and in the form of differentiation from its strongest competitor, John Deere.

How exactly has AGCO built this capability to be agile in the agricultural equipment marketplace? It has developed a framework of principles that enable breakthrough thinking in the company, including the following.

Get All Functions Involved

AGCO enlisted all areas of its business—from manufacturing to finance to dealer relations, sales, and marketing—to work together to develop breakthrough ideas. This cross-functional approach tapped into diverse skills and points of view. It also enabled AGCO to create its innovative "Fuse" technologies, which integrate telematics, data management systems, and auto guidance solutions that together have the potential to make farming much more productive and profitable.

Use Metaphors to Stimulate Thought

AGCO found that talking about the farm as what it was—a farm—made it difficult for employees to break out of their normal thought patterns regarding how they might solve customers' problems. The company decided to shift the conversation by speaking in the metaphor of a manufacturing facility. Using this metaphor changed the conversation, gave employees new language and ideas, and afforded the freedom to ask more revealing questions of the customers and of one another.

Look at the Whole Ecosystem

Because the research teams were on each farm for three weeks, they had plenty of time to observe the farmers' whole ecosystem—workers, dealers, extension agents, insurers, and other businesses that provided them with support. Building on the factory metaphor, they asked farmers questions in four areas:

- **Human resources.** What are your human resource problems? Is employee turnover higher than you would like? Why? What gaps do you see in worker skills? What challenges do you experience with employees?

- **Logistics.** How are machines used at each stage of the crop cycle—planning, seeding, application, harvesting, and storing? What can we do to optimize these? How do you transport the crop to and from market, and how do you store it? Who else is involved, and what data, communication, and paperwork are associated with these tasks?

- **Service.** How do you take care of your machinery? Do you use a dealer, or do you maintain it yourself? How much downtime do you have, and how do you optimize the way you run the machines? How much do you spend on service, and what are the challenges?

- **Finances.** How do you manage your finances, software, and data? What problems do you experience in managing these, and who else is involved? What machine data would be most helpful in managing finances and in making more money?

See for Yourself and Check Your Assumptions

When the AGCO team saw how farmers really lived and worked, they found that many of their original assumptions were incorrect—especially regarding the technology that farmers used to manage their business. As discussed in chapter 4, they discovered that cellular signals were far better in places like Kenya, South Africa, Tanzania, and Zambia than they were in North America. Use of mobile technologies for everyday activities like banking is far more pervasive in these regions than in North America. As a result, farmers were accustomed to using their mobile devices for everything, and expected to use them for managing the farm as well. They were, in fact, more ready to buy new technologies and more willing to spend money on value-producing technology upgrades than farmers in developed countries.

Use What's Already There

AGCO also discovered that farmers' most pressing issues had to do with optimizing and maintaining machines, maximizing uptime, managing product transport, and connecting to service providers and decision-support people. However, the company knew that farmers somewhere in the world had already begun developing solutions for many of these problems.

For example, when a sugarcane mill is down and not producing ethanol, it can cost the farmer thousands of dollars per hour. As a result, everything on the farm is geared to keeping that equipment running. But because no equipment manufacturers were offering telematics systems, Brazilian farmers had been asking their workers to use their phones to text activity codes (saying what they had been doing, and where) to a person in the office, who would use the codes to keep track of equipment and manpower utilization, and production rates.

AGCO determined that it could play an important and transformative role by making farming applications more compatible, by connecting the technologies, and by educating farmers and dealers about how to use technology to maintain and optimize equipment and farm operations.

Make a Different Choice Than Your Competitors

AGCO chose a different technology strategy than its competitors; it adopted an open approach, connecting and integrating technologies that many different developers had created. This allowed the company to offer more applications, more quickly and with less investment. Independent-minded farmers who wanted to use several brands of equipment and try diverse applications favored AGCO's open-technology philosophy.

Make Sure the Whole Channel Benefits from the Innovation

In addition to focusing on farmer productivity, AGCO also wanted to improve *dealer* profitability. The company is introducing new service offerings, such as service contracts which assure that the equipment will be fixed whenever it breaks down. It would have been risky for dealers to provide such a contract in the past. Now, dealers can use technology to proactively monitor the machine—allowing them to anticipate problems and service the equipment *before* it fails. AGCO benefits directly as farmers buy more add-on equipment such as telematics, while dealers gain new, high-margin, recurring revenue by providing services. Farmers benefit from greater machine uptime and efficiency. Everyone wins.

Techniques for Developing Breakthrough Thinking

Companies in other industries can apply the principles AGCO used to good effect. However, there are a variety of additional ways to stimulate breakthrough thinking in organizations. Consider trying the following techniques.

Assemble Grounded, Imaginative, and Cross-Functional Teams

When making a strategic decision to pursue a new opportunity or respond to a market trend or threat, you will want to assemble the best possible team to examine the facts, consider the options, and recommend a path forward. It's vital to assemble the right mix of employees and encourage debate and dissent among them.

Especially if you are considering a major change in strategy, you want to gather people from across your company's functions, levels, and geographies. A well-designed team doesn't just make better recommendations; it can build stronger organizational commitment to the action plan.

Keeping the team small will ensure more candid and effective discussion, and will keep everyone on their toes and engaged. However, you'll need to include a range of skills and expertise and to consider such factors as

- Who has the best insights on competition and on the customer?
- Who knows the nuts and bolts of how things really get done?
- Who is most creative and best able to imagine a new future?
- Who would benefit from the experience?
- Who has no preconceived notions and can provide a fresh perspective? (It's always helpful to have one "naive" person on the team.)
- Who has the interpersonal and process management skills to ensure that the team is effective?
- Which stakeholders' input and commitment are needed? Have key functions and geographic areas been represented? (And should we spread team meetings across several different geographic locations?)
- Who has the credibility to "sell" the group's decisions within the organization?

A breakthrough strategy, after all, results from observing the same market environment that all competitors see, but devising a new approach for capitalizing on it. A diverse team gives you your best shot at developing such a strategy.

Ensure that every team member sees personal benefit from serving on the team and that she knows her role. Team members serve an important function as diplomats, soliciting input from across the organization and gaining commitment to the plan going forward. The right team will enhance buy-in and increase your ability to combine assets and capabilities from across your entire organization.

Physical proximity—getting the team in the same room, at least for a period of time—is necessary as well. eBay, for example, gathers a group of ten to fifteen key people from different departments in a room for several days to focus on creating new products. The group is then divided into teams of four to seven people each. Using this approach, eBay teams can develop from four to six mock-up website designs in four days—far faster than the previous development protocol, which often took a full four months to develop a prototype.[1]

When team members are physically gathered together, they can make decisions much more quickly, creatively, and rigorously. The team often arrives at totally different outcomes than they would if they worked via email and conference calls. When they are in the same room, team members can work silently and independently on their respective work streams if they so desire. But when they need feedback, information, a shot of creativity, or just an emotional boost, they can speak to another team member immediately. It often takes just five minutes to clear up a question face-to-face that might take days via email. It's especially important to use this approach when team members come from different cultures and time zones, or speak different languages.

Ask New Questions

Asking provocative, specific questions can jostle you out of ruts, expose outdated or errant assumptions, and help generate truly new ideas. The questions here may or may not work well for the situation you are facing, but they give you an idea of the *types* of questions you should be asking to jump-start creative thinking.

- What is a totally different way of reaching our goals? For example, instead of shipping finished products to customers, we could ship components, so that customers can customize a solution to fit their needs.

- What can we decrease, or stop doing altogether? For example, AT&T stopped requiring customers to enter a new twenty-four-month service contract to get a new cell phone with no up-front cost.

- Can we reverse any element of our solution or do it in the opposite way? For example, National Rental Car reversed the car-selection process. Instead of selecting cars for its customers, it allowed them to walk to the lot and drive away in the car they liked best.

- What would we do differently if we could develop any capabilities we wanted by waving a magic wand? For example, what if we could instantly develop a sales channel in Asia?

- What would we do if we knew that our current business would dwindle to zero within the next two years? For example, we could place small bets on promising new lines of business, with the hope of ensuring long-term company growth.

- What might technology allow us to do in two years that is impossible now? For example, autonomous vehicle technology may allow us to introduce new products for drivers who are no longer fully engaged in the driving process.

Challenge Existing Assumptions and Ways of Doing Things

When I lived in Kuala Lumpur, Malaysia, I'd frequently see entire families—a dad, a mom, and two kids—riding a single motorbike through the city, usually without helmets. Imagine how unsafe it was. Indeed, the number of road traffic deaths per capita in this and other developing countries is more than twice that in the United States and Europe.[2]

Tata, India's fourth-largest automaker and the owner of Jaguar and Land Rover, set out to help solve this problem by asking a new question: How can we make a car that can be marketed for only $2,000 (100,000 rupees), so that families who could previously only afford a motorbike can trade up?

Tata engineers started completely from scratch when designing the ultra-low-cost Nano car, questioning every assumption about how a car should be shaped, constructed, and sold. The company used plastic body parts, connected with adhesives instead of rivets and welding. It employed a two-cylinder engine and only one windshield wiper. The seats were not even adjustable. The car's distribution channel was revolutionary as well, enlisting people in small businesses, such as local cloth-sellers, as distributors.

The result was the least-expensive mass-produced automobile in the world—truly within financial reach for families traveling by motor scooter. What an accomplishment—to create something so new and different that it could fundamentally change thousands of families' lifestyle, safety, and comfort. This result came from challenging assumptions and conventional wisdom. Although the car didn't fare as well as hoped in its originally intended target market—people trading up from motorbikes—it did better than expected with people wishing to buy a second car or a car for their parents or children. It was a bold experiment and learning opportunity for Tata, and subsequent cars will build on the innovations developed for this model.

Develop Multiple Alternatives

Take the time to develop several substantially different alternatives for addressing the opportunities and threats you see. Often, companies fall into the trap of considering only two options: yes and no. By boiling down a major corporate strategic decision into a simple, binary decision, they fail to see other creative and potentially superior options. Either we enter this market or we don't. Either we divest the underperforming business or we don't. We consider a single alternative, develop one pro forma—and the boss, executive committee, or board decides yea or nay.

Working to develop *several* dramatically different strategic alternatives can catalyze new thinking. Even if you ultimately reject the alternatives you come up with, they strengthen the action plan you eventually develop.

Figure 6.1 provides a framework for thinking through the elements of your business model that could be changed so as to adjust for, or take advantage of, the changes you see in your market.

Check the Endpoints and Fill the Whole Space

When working to develop new ideas, it's often remarkably helpful to create a simple sketch labeling the "dimensions" of the alternatives. This allows you to readily see what might be missing.

Let's imagine that you have just invented a marvelous new machine—say, a 3D printer that can fabricate products on demand, once it receives a "print job" from an employee. The machine is amazing, and many types of businesses could benefit from having one. However, it requires periodic service, and because prospective customers are not familiar with its many uses, you expect that a face-to-face sales call will be required to complete the sale. To be profitable, you will need to set up cost-effective service systems and sales channels. The trouble is, you've found that the service levels you can provide profitably to large customers in urban areas are cost-prohibitive for small customers in rural areas.

As illustrated in Figure 6.2, in designing your sales and service model, you could select two dimensions to look at: customer size and urban-versus-rural geography. By simply labeling them on a page and filling in how you will serve each of these customer types differently, you can develop an initial basis for customer segmentation and generate ideas about how the business model might differ for each segment.

When you "check the endpoints"—that is, look at the extreme cases at the edges of the figure—you can easily come up with new business model ideas. For example, the "mega-urban" customers in the top right of Figure 6.2 are extremely large and

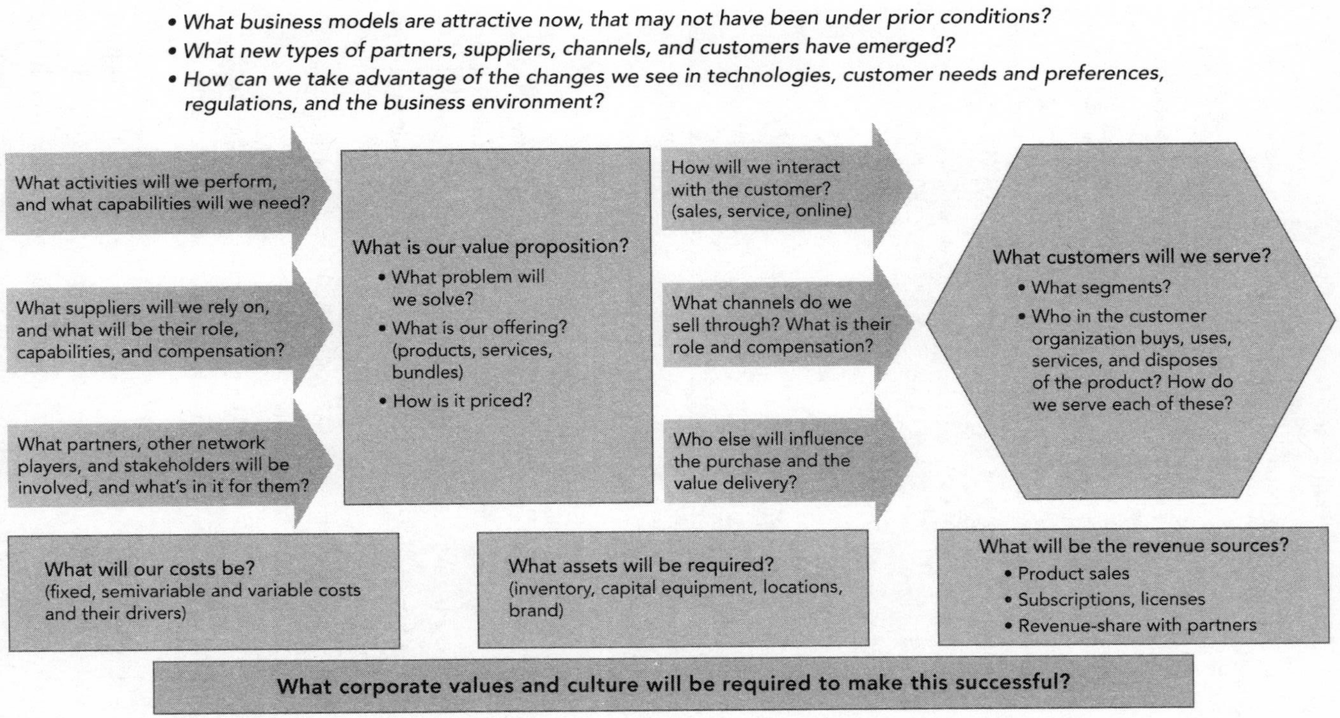

- *What business models are attractive now, that may not have been under prior conditions?*
- *What new types of partners, suppliers, channels, and customers have emerged?*
- *How can we take advantage of the changes we see in technologies, customer needs and preferences, regulations, and the business environment?*

What activities will we perform, and what capabilities will we need?

What suppliers will we rely on, and what will be their role, capabilities, and compensation?

What partners, other network players, and stakeholders will be involved, and what's in it for them?

What is our value proposition?
- What problem will we solve?
- What is our offering? (products, services, bundles)
- How is it priced?

How will we interact with the customer? (sales, service, online)

What channels do we sell this through? What is their role and compensation?

Who else will influence the purchase and the value delivery?

What customers will we serve?
- What segments?
- Who in the customer organization buys, uses, services, and disposes of the product? How do we serve each of these?

What will our costs be? (fixed, semivariable and variable costs and their drivers)

What assets will be required? (inventory, capital equipment, locations, brand)

What will be the revenue sources?
- Product sales
- Subscriptions, licenses
- Revenue-share with partners

What corporate values and culture will be required to make this successful?

Figure 6.1 Setili Thought-Starter for Business Model Innovation

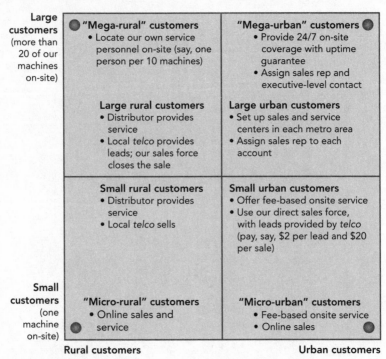

Figure 6.2 Checking the Endpoints and Filling the Whole Space (Example)

in dense urban markets. You can cost-effectively offer them an ultra-premium service, with 24/7 personnel on-site coverage and an uptime guarantee. The "micro-rural" customers in the lower left of the figure, however, might be most profitably served by an online-only model.

When you "fill the whole space" by examining the cases in the center of the figure, you might think of ways to offer sales and service by partnering with distributors for service or by using local telecommunications companies to provide leads or even to sell the product.

Customer size and geography are but two of the dimensions we could have chosen for this exercise. Experiment with picking other dimensions (in this example, customer sophistication, likely frequency of using the machine, or the degree to which customers purchase other equipment made by your company might make sense) and see what you find when you "check the endpoints and fill the whole space."

Innovate by Eliminating

Don't fall victim to the temptation to add features, services, products, and markets every year. In fact, it's a good idea to assess how you can differentiate by *taking away* features.

IKEA is a prime example of a brand that engages in "innovating by eliminating." The well-known Swedish furniture retailer broke with tradition by doing away with traditionally "standard" features like in-store service, delivery, and assembly. As anyone who has visited IKEA knows, the stores are almost entirely self-service. Yet IKEA provides a distinctive, enjoyable shopping experience by offering clever, inspiring displays and ready availability of tape measures and notepads. You feel almost as if you've visited an amusement park.

Shoppers typically carry the products home themselves—though there is the option to pay extra for delivery and assembly—but IKEA packages items into compact boxes that fit easily into almost any vehicle. Customers perform the job of construction, but IKEA's simple, stick-figure instructions make the process fun, like assembling a LEGO toy. In fact, the *Journal of Consumer Psychology* reports that customers like their product more, and are even willing to pay more, if they assemble their IKEA product themselves.[3]

My first experience with IKEA occurred when we lived in Kuala Lumpur and brought home a new dresser and assembled it with our young daughter. She was only two years old, but was very excited to see the pieces emerge from the flat box and transform into the shape of her new piece of furniture, with drawers that she could fill. This created an enduring and positive family memory—tied indelibly to the IKEA brand.

Whereas other furniture stores emphasize their products' durability and timelessness, IKEA makes us think of furniture as a fashion accessory—something we can use for a while and then replace. By taking away features, IKEA creates a compelling customer experience and keeps prices amazingly low.

Give Team Members Time to Think Independently

Studies have shown that people think better independently than in a group. In a *New York Times* article, Susan Cain, author of *Quiet: The Power of Introverts in a World That Can't Stop Talking,* cites the work of psychologists Mihaly Csikszentmihalyi and Gregory Feist: "Research strongly suggests that people are more creative when they enjoy privacy and freedom from interruption. And the most spectacularly creative people in many fields are often introverted ... They're extroverted enough to exchange and advance ideas, but see themselves as independent and individualistic. They're not joiners by nature."[4]

The key is to harness the strength of individual creativity while also exploiting the power of group interaction. During his weekly two-hour meetings with the company's senior leadership team and engineers, Amazon CEO Jeff Bezos requires attendees who want to share an idea with the group to write a six-page memo (no PowerPoints allowed!) clarifying their recommendations and the rationale for it. The entire group is then allowed twenty to twenty-five minutes of quiet time at the beginning of the meeting to read and absorb the memo.[5]

Use Open Innovation to Gain Ideas from the Outside

Using open innovation techniques can give you access to a pool of thinkers that would otherwise be very difficult to tap into.

Procter & Gamble was one of the early adopters of the open innovation concept. More than half of new product initiatives at P&G involve significant collaboration with outside innovators. The company posts R&D problems on a website called Connect+Develop, where thousands of external innovators—including companies, individual entrepreneurs, and university researchers—compete to come up with the best solution. The program was responsible for breakthrough products including Swiffer Dusters, Mr. Clean Magic Erasers, Tide Pods, and Olay Regenerist face cream.

Beiersdorf, German maker of Aquaphor, Eucerin, Nivea, and other leading health and beauty brands, uses its Pearlfinder program to attract potential partners—suppliers, inventors, academics, and others, all around the world—to attack its biggest technical and product improvement challenges. Potential partners are vetted and sign nondisclosure agreements before they become part of the Pearlfinder community and before any confidential information is shared. Beiersdorf prides itself on treating contributors fairly and making sure the relationship is a true partnership; the company is looking for long-term arrangements with the best and most innovative partners in the world.[6]

With its $200 million Ecomagination Challenge, General Electric has partnered with top venture capital firms—including Emerald Technology Ventures and Kleiner Perkins Caufield & Byers—to reach out to businesses, entrepreneurs, innovators, and students to find the best solutions for a broad set of challenges. The three challenges addressed to date are powering the grid, powering the home, and low carbon ANZ (Australia and New Zealand). Winners receive a cash award of $100,000 plus a capital pledge from GE to invest in their promising start-ups and ideas. The program generated strong and immediate interest and ideas from all around the world, and more than five thousand ideas were submitted within the first six months. To date, GE and the venture capital firms have made more than $134 million in investments through this program.[7]

Visualize Early and Use Prototypes

Prototyping is a powerful tool for building out concepts and testing them with different audiences. It is a way to think through how each alternative would actually work and be used. As you start to build the prototype, you make decisions about what goes where, what connects to what, and how customers will interact with your solution—whether it's a new physical product, an online or mobile solution, a new business model, or a service. Restaurant chains have prototype restaurants, and online entities test new concepts daily in A/B tests. Any company can pilot new concepts on a small scale to test customer and internal response and to gain experience with the operational aspects of the product or service.

A crude prototype is often better than a sophisticated one, because it invites suggestions and makes it OK to tear up and reinvent whatever you've done. In contrast, a slick, fully formed prototype tends to bring mainly praise, because viewers are often hesitant to criticize an idea that the team has already worked on extensively. You therefore want to produce new prototypes *often* throughout your innovation process. Even a set of PowerPoint slides using images you've found online can help your audience to imagine the alternatives you are exploring and to offer helpful suggestions. Using this process, you can springboard off your initial concepts to generate further creative ideas.

eBay uses a prototyping technique called "previsualizing" (preVIZ in eBay speak), borrowed from the film industry. Film directors use this process to visualize complex scenes so that they can experiment with different treatments before investing in expensive production. eBay designers partner with internal business teams to create mock-ups of new business ideas and to present these ideas to its clients, such as the consumer products companies that sell on eBay. The technique enables eBay to flesh out and visualize an idea without actually implementing it.[8]

The company can then test, build on, modify, or discard more ideas—leading to a better end result.

eBay also uses the "headlines" technique, in which an innovation team comes up with the headline and executive summary of an article about their breakthrough idea to be written in the fictitious future. The team decides when the headline would be published, what the news would be, who would be quoted, what the impact of the news would be, and why it matters. This technique encourages the team to visualize a potential future scenario and to bring it to life for others.[9]

When Google Glass was first developed, the company released early versions to ten thousand people—Explorers in Google-speak—who wished to test the product. Google selected the Explorers from a pool of applicants, asked them to try the product, then collected ideas on how they used it. After an initial testing period, each of these Explorers had the opportunity to invite up to three friends into the program. Each new Explorer would have to pay $1,500 for the Google Glass product, but would play a role in shaping how the product evolved.

Leverage Ideas from Outside Your Industry

When you observe companies in industries and markets outside your own, what do you see that you can copy, leverage, or learn from?

For example, even if you are in a totally different business than Google, you may be able to learn from its rapid pace of innovation; its diverse, ever-evolving product line; and its pricing models, which provide almost every product other than advertising (and there are many) for free.

Table 6.1 is an example of how a company in the industrial products business might look to Walmart as an exemplar, even though the two companies are in different industries and are of vastly different size. The first column lists some of Walmart's

Table 6.1 Using Walmart as an Exemplar (Example: Industrial Products Company)

Walmart Characteristics	Example	Benefit	How Can We Apply This to Our Business?
Culture of austerity and efficiency	Bare-bones offices and strict 15-minute meetings with vendors	Low cost is a way of life for employees. This helps keep expenses from growing every year.	We send mixed messages. The executive suite is gold-plated, but we ask the plants to cut costs every year. We should consider high-visibility ways to cut headquarters cost (without cutting back on staff).
Very consistent brand focus on low prices, decade after decade	Walmart really stands behind its tagline "Save Money, Live Better." For example, prices on produce are often 30% lower than in other stores.	People build the habit of shopping at Walmart due to the low prices. The focus on price allows Walmart to reduce labor costs, because shoppers don't expect much service.	We've positioned our brand in three different ways over the last 10 years. Let's settle on one and stick with it. Then we can design our business systems to make sure we deliver on the brand promise, instead of vacillating each year on priorities.
Success with store brands	Ol' Roy dog food is the best-selling dog food in the world.	High profit for company, low price for customer—good combination!	We could offer product on a private-label basis to distributors in geographies we don't plan to serve. This would allow us to increase sales with no investment in sales and marketing.
Rigorous procurement processes, demanding of vendors	Clothing sizes are consistent across different brands and manufacturers.	Size standardization is a unique benefit versus other department stores.	Our customers are confused by the way product specification parameters vary from product to product. Some of our competitors have simpler systems for specifying products. Customers would buy more if we could create simpler ways for them to specify and order products.

(Continued)

Table 6.1 Using Walmart as an Exemplar (Example: Industrial Products Company) (*Continued*)

Walmart Characteristics	Example	Benefit	How Can We Apply This to Our Business?
Invest in infrastructure to reduce cost	Walmart has invested in world-class information technology and logistics systems.	These have been critical to Walmart's success as low-price leader.	Our IT and logistics systems are good, but our sales and customer service costs are still worse than average for our industry. Should we invest to bring these costs down?

strengths; the second lists an example of how this strength is manifested; the third lists the benefits Walmart enjoys as a result of the strength; and the fourth asks, "How can we apply this to our business?" You can prepare the first three columns ahead of time, and fill out the fourth in a group setting as a brainstorming exercise.

Exemplars abound. Consider Apple's app developer community, elegant packaging, distinctive retail experience, and the way they create customer evangelists. Consider how Amazon suggests new products personalized to each customer's taste; how valuable its product reviews are; how its Prime memberships (which offer free two-day shipping) have revolutionized customer buying habits; how it has helped create the electronic publishing business; and how its subscription-based sales of consumable products like groceries and supplies have changed the way people buy.

Focus on a Specific Customer or Customer Segment

When I travel to Houston, I stay in an area that has nine hotels crowded into a two-thousand-foot-long stretch of road. All are national brands that I trust and have stayed in many times in other locales, and I've stayed in at least three of the nine hotels in this neighborhood. How do I choose where to book my next reservation when traveling to this area? Price is not a factor, given that most of the nine are priced in a tight band between $96 and $136. The decision comes down to which guest experience fits my needs better.

Homewood Suites must have had someone like me in mind when they designed their offering. When I travel for business, I like to exercise after a day spent in meetings, then eat a simple, quick, and healthy dinner and do some late-night work in my room. To fit all this in, I need a fast, convenient dining option.

An increasing number of brands—including Homewood Suites' parent company, Hilton—are discontinuing room service because it is complex and costly to run. However, Homewood Suites *does* offer a very attractive combination of several other dining options. If I arrive hungry late at night, I can purchase a packaged or frozen entree from the twenty-four-hour convenience store in the lobby and cook it in my fully equipped in-suite kitchen. If I'm going to be staying several days, I can give the hotel a grocery list, and it will stock my refrigerator, with no markups on price. If I'm in the mood for variety, I can order from an extensive delivery menu provided by an outsourced service called Order Inn. And finally, my personal favorite—I can enjoy a free dinner between 5:30 and 7:30 every Monday through Thursday, right in the hotel. Business travelers like me want to feel at home when they travel, and Homewood Suites has gotten as close as I've seen to providing a homelike hotel experience.

Hotel chains have many constituencies to please. They must satisfy a variety of business and leisure guests, and they must also provide a brand recipe that is operationally feasible and profitable for the franchisees. Each time a franchisee purchases a piece of real estate, he has a choice of many brands to locate there. Therefore, keeping franchisees happy is just as important as keeping guests happy, if not more so.

The Homewood Suites free dinner appeals to me as a guest because it saves me time. It appeals to franchisees because it's a far less costly dining option than providing room service. The free meals are centrally planned by the chain and are designed to be prepared by only one or two employees in a very limited kitchen space. The cost is very controllable, and adds up to only a few dollars per guest per day.

With competitors offering so many different amenities—from yoga mats to business centers and laundry facilities to extensive pillow selections—chains need to pick a package of amenities that they can manage consistently between different properties, but that will create a distinctive and memorable customer experience. Homewood Suites took a very creative approach by combining a set of amenities that accomplishes both of these objectives.

In an intensely competitive location like the one I described in Houston, choosing the right package of benefits to appeal to a specific type of traveler is critical to survival. Homewood Suites must have chosen wisely, because the hotel is one of only two in this locale (out of nine) with a rating of four-and-a-half or more on TripAdvisor—and it is often sold out when other hotels in the area have plenty of vacancies.

In Conclusion

Building an organization that can react quickly and decisively to changes in the business environment depends on its people's ability to generate creative alternatives and breakthrough strategies. This chapter has provided examples of successful companies that have found ways to accomplish this consistently and with great success. As you look for ways to create your own breakthrough strategies and ideas, consider implementing the following approaches:

- **Assemble grounded, imaginative, and cross-functional teams.** Ensure that they comprise diverse groups of experts and creative thinkers from across your organization who are specifically asked to develop strategies for addressing emerging opportunities.

- **Ask new questions.** Asking provocative, specific questions can shake up your thinking and help you question long-held assumptions. Ask, for example: What can we increase, decrease, reverse, separate, or bundle? How can we reduce cost to one-tenth of its current level, or deliver twice as fast? What totally new value can we offer the customer?

- **Develop multiple alternatives.** Develop a number of alternatives for addressing your opportunity, and make sure each is substantially different from the others. Forcing the team to come up with diverse alternatives ensures that they don't stick only with safe and predictable choices.

- **Look at the whole ecosystem.** It's not enough to look at just part of your customer's organization or ecosystem. To be ready to act intelligently, quickly, and decisively, you must observe your customer's entire ecosystem—including customers, suppliers, partners, and employees.

- **Make a different choice than your competitors.** When sailboat racers want to make a bold move to gain advantage over the competition, they look for better wind elsewhere on the racecourse, and tack away. You can do the same by choosing a different strategy than your competitors.

- **Check the endpoints and fill the whole space.** When generating new ideas, it's often remarkably helpful to create a simple sketch labeling the "dimensions" of the alternatives available to you and your organization. This approach can allow you to readily see what might be missing.

- **Innovate by eliminating.** Instead of constantly piling on new product or service features—which may increase cost with no increase in customer satisfaction—consider how you can differentiate by *taking away* features.

- **Give team members time to think independently.** People think better independently than in a group, and can be more creative when they enjoy privacy and freedom from interruption.

- **Use open innovation to gain ideas from the outside.** Tap into knowledge and viewpoints that don't exist within your company by sharing your innovation challenges with other companies, entrepreneurs, university researchers, and others.
- **Use metaphors to stimulate thought.** Using a metaphor—such as AGCO's view of a farm as a manufacturing facility—stimulates thought and affords the freedom to ask entirely new and more revealing questions of customers and of one another.
- **Visualize early and use prototypes.** Produce new prototypes *often* throughout your innovation process. This enables you to see how each alternative would actually work and be used, and to test your concepts with different audiences. Present multiple concepts and use an iterative approach.
- **Leverage ideas from outside your industry.** There are lessons to be learned from observing companies in industries and markets outside your own. What do you see that you can copy, leverage, or learn from?
- **Focus on a specific customer or customer segment.** You can't be everything to everyone, and you really shouldn't try. Have a specific customer type in mind when you design your offering.

Chapter Seven

Manage Uncertainty

Be Courageous, Anticipate What Might Happen, and Address Risks Head-On

No matter what business or industry you are in, risks exist. Competitors enter the market, customer tastes change, new technologies appear, and market prices can take dramatic and damaging swings. The future is never certain; but in some industries, it is profoundly *uncertain.*

Good strategy nearly always involves a bet, so leaders must become comfortable with making decisions in precarious environments. They must also become adept at quickly and decisively managing risks related to demand, competition, and their organization's ability to develop new capabilities.

When Elon Musk started SpaceX and Tesla Motors, he had a realistic view of his odds of success, assessing them at "a fair bit less than 50 percent."[1] Yet he has made both ventures very successful. Tesla is the first successful new U.S. car company in fifty years, and the company's Model S is the best-selling vehicle in more of the twenty-five wealthiest communities in the United States than any other vehicle.[2] SpaceX created the first commercial spacecraft in history to shuttle cargo to and from the International Space

Station, and now provides cargo transportation for NASA, which retired its own space shuttle, as well as for other customers. Both endeavors have so far proven to be worth the risk.

Musk was also founder of Zip2 and PayPal, and now serves simultaneously as CEO of both Solar City and Tesla Motors. He has taken bold chances at multiple points in his career—and even has his sights set on colonizing Mars someday. Though one of the most innovative and courageous leaders of our time, Musk retains a grounded sense of what's doable. "Wishful thinking is one of the most profound human failings, and the major reason why people adhere so strongly to wrong ideas. This doesn't mean that you can't be optimistic. You simply have to be realistic as well," Musk says in David S. Kidder's book *The Startup Playbook*.[3]

Musk has avoided three mistakes that I have observed other companies make in managing risk and uncertainty:

Mistake number 1: Taking no action. Executives often fail to make a strategic move because they are uncomfortable with the risks or cannot agree on whether it's worth the potential reward. When the rest of the smartphone industry moved to touchscreen technology, BlackBerry (then called RIM) stuck with keyboards for far too long. BlackBerry's market share plummeted as a result of this and other missteps, and the company found itself struggling to survive.

Mistake number 2: Engaging in "me-tooism." This occurs when a company takes the "safe" route by waiting until a competitor has succeeded with a new strategic choice, then following the competitor's moves. Almost every industry has a few companies that subscribe to this fast-follower approach. They avoid difficult strategic decisions, but find themselves with an undifferentiated offering and mediocre results. For example, auction websites auction.com, eBid.net, ePier, and others like them have not attained nearly the level of market penetration nor success as eBay—the company that pioneered online auctions.

Mistake number 3: Being overconfident. Companies make a bold move, but fail to adequately identify and manage the inherent risks. They want to invest and grow, so their financial projections assume that many things will go right. I see this time and again as companies enter new markets but fail to manage the risks, such as customer and channel acceptance. Hewlett-Packard's failed introduction of the TouchPad tablet in 2011—a product it pulled only forty-nine days after launching it—provides an apt example.

In this chapter, we'll consider how to make decisions in an uncertain environment and how to maximize the chance of success when undertaking a risky strategic move. Let's first take a look at Tesla Motors to explore Elon Musk's approach to managing risk.

How Tesla Motors Succeeded, and Managed Risk

Musk knew that for electric-powered vehicles to be successful, his company would need to build an attractive, fun to drive, safe car that had a range—the distance the car could be driven before a recharge or refueling—equal to gasoline-powered vehicles.

The incumbent auto manufacturers had not achieved this. Although Nissan, Ford, and others had poured many millions of dollars (and yen) into development, the cars that resulted—such as the Nissan Leaf and the Ford Focus Electric—looked and drove like economy cars. In addition, their limited range—around eighty miles in ideal conditions—made them fine for daily commutes around town but largely unsuitable for long-distance travel.

Despite the challenges of bringing a new vehicle to market—much less one that is not powered by traditional fossil fuels—Musk is passionate about proving the commercial viability of electric vehicles. He understood the risks of pursuing his goal, and set out to address each one of them.

Design Your Strategy to Maximize Learning

Musk's strategy was designed for learning. Whereas competitors such as the Leaf and the Focus Electric started at the mass-market end of the price spectrum, Tesla entered the market at the high end, starting with a high-cost (more than $100,000 for a base model), high-performance (0–60 mph in 3.7 seconds), but intentionally low-volume sports car: the Tesla Roadster. The company then moved on to a midpriced ($62,400 for a base model), medium-volume luxury sedan, the Tesla Model S. A "mass-market" Model E is planned to go on sale in 2016 or 2017, priced in the neighborhood of $40,000.[4] This strategy of starting with a low-volume, expensive model and gradually moving to lower price points enabled the company to learn about design, manufacturing, and customer response while intentionally offering a low-volume model.

Think about what initial steps would enable you to learn what you need to learn to succeed when moving into risky strategic territory. Figure 7.1 provides a framework for considering some potential learning objectives.

Starting out with the low-volume Roadster enabled Tesla to work with Panasonic and other suppliers to develop the battery system and other components—a process shown in the top left box, "Develop external capability." It provided an opportunity to iron out design features and manufacturing processes, and allowed the company to recruit the talent it would need to expand into higher-volume models (the bottom left box, where internal capability comes into play). Tesla's experience with the Roadster also provided valuable information about consumer preferences, thereby enabling external acceptance (the top right box). Finally, it provided evidence to employees, partners, and investors that the battle was winnable—that Tesla could design great-looking, high-performance, sought-after electric vehicles (bottom right box).

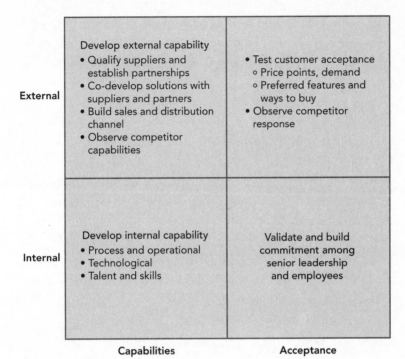

Figure 7.1 Creating a Learning Strategy: Objectives of Initial Steps, Experiments, Trials, and Pilots

As you develop your own learning strategy, ask:

- What do you need to learn to make your next move successful?
- How can you design your strategy to meet these learning objectives?

Manage Technology Risk

Musk adopted a technology that had become pervasive in laptops, phones, and other consumer electronics, but that had not been proved cost effective for use in vehicles: the compact, rechargeable lithium-ion battery. He then focused on bringing that technology's cost down to a level that was practical for mass-market vehicles. This was a strategic gamble, but it paid off, as the Tesla battery provides far greater range than other electric cars—250 to 300 miles, versus a more typical 80 to 100 miles—and much more impressive power and performance, compared to previous technologies.

However, the battery is heavy. So Musk's company set out to offset the weight by making the entire body and most of the chassis out of aluminum. (Key areas are made of high-strength steel to enhance occupant safety.) Although aluminum is expensive, it is far lighter than steel *and* provides better protection in an accident because it absorbs more energy as it crushes, thereby protecting the car's occupants.

When considering new, or new-to-you, technologies as part of your breakthrough strategy, ask yourself the questions outlined in Table 7.1. We see the way Tesla answered these questions and solved the related problems here.

Manage Customer-Demand Risk

Even with a great vehicle design, there was still a significant risk that consumer demand for Tesla's electric vehicles would not materialize. After all, most electric cars were not meeting their sales goals at the time that the Model S was released—despite the fact that they were offered by well-known brands with strong dealer networks and were priced in the affordable $30,000 range.

To address this risk, Musk and the Tesla team identified two major consumer concerns that might stop customers from buying, and set out to directly address them.

Customer concern #1: Resale value. The first concern is consumers' fear that the Tesla's resale value might not be as good as that of a conventional car. To allay this concern, Tesla cleverly designed a financing program that lets buyers return a Model S after three years and receive a guaranteed residual—essentially a trade-in price—pegged to the value of a Mercedes-Benz S-Class. Tesla buyers also have the option of simply paying off the rest of their loan and keeping the vehicle.

Table 7.1 How Can You Employ New Technologies to Reduce Risk and Create Breakthroughs?

Questions to Ask Yourself	Your Answers	Tesla Example
CURRENT LIMITATIONS AND OBJECTIVES: What objectives could you potentially achieve, or what limitations could you overcome, through technology advancement? • Cost • Performance • Speed and flexibility	1. _____ 2. _____ 3. _____ 4. _____	The battery technologies that incumbent auto companies were using provided insufficient vehicle range.
POTENTIAL SOLUTIONS: What technologies, or technology enhancements, could potentially be employed?	1. _____ 2. _____ 3. _____ 4. _____	Tesla saw potential in the small lithium-ion battery, which could be both less dangerous and less expensive than batteries used by other electric vehicle manufacturers.
RISKS: What risks do these potential new technologies present?	1. _____ 2. _____ 3. _____ 4. _____	To commercialize the small lithium-ion battery, Tesla had to figure out how to wire thousands of AA-size cells together within the car, and how to keep each cell cool.
DEVELOPMENT PATH: What development and learning will be required to employ these technologies?	1. _____ 2. _____ 3. _____ 4. _____	Tesla developed an initial version of its battery technology for the Roadster, then improved on this design in the Model S, bringing costs down to one-half the Roadster level, on a per-kilowatt-hour basis.*

*Kevin Bullis, "How Tesla Is Driving Electric Car Innovation," *MIT Technology Review*, August 7, 2013, http://www.technologyreview.com/news/516961/how-tesla-is-driving-electric-car-innovation/.

Of course, some potential buyers might still worry that the guarantee would be worthless if Tesla failed as a company. To address this, Musk went on record saying, "No matter what happens to Tesla . . . I will stand by the residual value if Tesla cannot, with all the assets at my disposal." *Forbes* estimates Musk's net worth at over $6 billion—so his personal guarantee carries weight with consumers.

Customer concern #2: Range. The second major concern of potential buyers was "range anxiety." That is, what would happen if you were unable to make it to a charging station when on a long-distance trip? To address this, Tesla is installing conveniently located "Superchargers" where Tesla owners can recharge their cars at no cost. (You can check out the map at http://www.teslamotors.com/supercharger to envision trips you might take.) An hour—enough time to stop for lunch—provides a full charge. Even just twenty minutes to stretch your legs and get a cup of coffee provides three hours of drive time.

Already, more than 99 percent of California Tesla owners, and 87 percent of Oregon and Washington owners, are within two hundred miles of a Supercharger, and the East Coast, the Chicago area, and Texas are also well served. Tesla's Supercharger coverage is expected to reach 98 percent of the U.S. population by the end of 2015. The rollout of Superchargers in Europe is on a similar schedule, and other locations, such as China, are in the works.

You can foresee challenges that come up in your own situation by answering the questions outlined in Table 7.2.

Leverage Your Assets and Partnerships to Manage Risk

Tesla's free charging at Superchargers is a compelling offer; imagine being able to drive coast to coast without spending a cent on fuel, for the life of the vehicle. How is the company able to do this? Well, in addition to being the CEO of Tesla, Musk is also the CEO of SolarCity—a company that designs and installs leased solar panels for homes and businesses. Having SolarCity solar panels on each Supercharger station makes the station capable of putting more energy back into the grid than Tesla drivers consume by recharging their cars.[5]

Working with partners and leveraging the assets in your network, as Musk did in this example, are critical steps for managing risk and moving any venture along faster. Consider

Table 7.2 Developing an Action Plan to Address
Customer-Demand Risk

What Might Keep Your Customers from Buying?	Your Action Plan	Tesla Example
Cost-related concerns (for example, costs related to buying, using, or disposing of your product) 1. _____ 2. _____ 3. _____		Tesla addressed customer concerns about resale value through a buy-back program.
Value-related concerns (for example, ease of use, performance, value in use) 1. _____ 2. _____ 3. _____		Tesla allayed worries about range by installing Superchargers along major travel routes.
Marketing and channel-related concerns (for example, do customers know about your product and its benefits? Is your product available when and where they need it?) 1. _____ 2. _____ 3. _____		Tesla had no dealer network, so the company elected to sell direct-to-consumer, online and via company-owned retail stores located in shopping malls.

what assets and partnerships you can leverage to implement
your own breakthrough strategy more effectively, or to mitigate
potential risks.

Manage Competitive Risk: Think from the Ground Up to Develop a Differentiated Offering

Elon Musk has no trouble competing against established giants
like Nissan, Ford, and GM in auto manufacturing, GE in solar
power, and NASA in space travel—because large companies like
these tend to innovate incrementally. For the most part, they
haven't mastered the "ground-up" thinking that leads to truly
breakthrough ideas.

Rather than looking at what already exists and trying to tweak it, Musk innovates by starting with the fundamental truths—such as the basic laws of physics—and reasoning up from there. This philosophy has been a major factor in his success in multiple, disparate industries, from financial services to space travel to cars to solar power. When, for instance, he saw that the amount of fuel and material required to lift a full load of cargo to the International Space Station was only 1 percent of what NASA was actually spending on the space shuttle, he figured that he could do the job for less—and then set out to do just that. His SpaceX craft will soon carry twice the payload of the former NASA shuttle, for about one-tenth the cost per pound.[6]

Tesla Motors did something similar by adapting lithium-ion batteries for use in vehicles. The company diverged from standard industry practice by placing the batteries low and flat in the car. Because the battery case is part of the car's structural frame, batteries take up no passenger and cargo space—and more important, it makes for a low center of gravity and a better-handling, safer vehicle. Combined with the instant responsiveness of the electric power train, this makes for a thrilling driver experience.

To think from the ground up, ask yourself these questions:

- In what arenas have your own and your organization's thinking become constrained by established practices, beliefs, and norms?
- Given the strategic problems and opportunities that you face, what would it mean to "think from the ground up"?
- If you were to reduce your problem to its fundamental truths, what new and different solutions might your company produce?

Be the Best at Something

Musk's ability to directly manage the risks he identified and to employ bottom-up thinking resulted in a truly breakthrough design. He proved that it was possible to make an electric vehicle so high performing, safe, and attractive that consumers would find it irresistible.

Then he went further—to make sure that the Tesla Model S would be recognized as the very best on multiple metrics. *Road and Track* wrote that the Tesla Model S is the most important car in United States history, and *Consumer Reports* gave the car a 99 out of a 100-point rating, the highest score in six years and matched only once before, by the Lexus LS600. The National Highway Traffic Safety Administration (NHTSA) gave the Model S its highest rating on every measure, enabling Tesla to boast of "the highest safety rating in America."[7]

At times, becoming the very best required Musk to overcome substantial internal opposition. For example, his goal of achieving the lowest drag coefficient in the industry required unswerving attention to aerodynamic details. Musk even insisted that Tesla engineers design the door handles to retract when the car was in motion and move back out when the driver approached. This engineering challenge meant an added expense. The handles had to be strong enough to break through a layer of ice but sensitive enough to stop moving when a child's finger got in the way.

Musk related in a 2013 interview with *Fortune*, "There were numerous conversations where I had pushback from the engineers. And it's not like they were saying, 'Oh, this is a challenge.' [It was] more like, 'This is the stupidest thing ever.' But we did it in the end, and yes, I think it's cool—one of the car's signature features."[8]

Although you don't have to win awards to be the best at something, you do need to define what will make your product or service truly distinctive—and *for whom*. If you are merely at par with the competition, you will find yourself competing on price, squeaking by on thin margins, and struggling to grow.

To determine what you will be best at, ask these questions:

- For what target customer groups is your product or service ideally suited?

- In what ways will this target customer regard you as the very best?
- How will you demonstrate this superiority, and spread the word in a credible way, to grow sales and earn a price premium?

What Should We Learn from Elon Musk?

Although Elon Musk is willing to take risks to achieve something important to him, he risks only *what he can afford to risk*. Further, and perhaps more instructive for all of us, Musk identifies specific risks and assumptions quite clearly and then implements a plan to address each. Range too low? Use more powerful, lithium-ion batteries, and install solar-powered Supercharger stations all over the world. Car too heavy? Make it out of a lighter material. Concerns about resale value? Here's a buy-back guarantee. Worried about safety? Put in the effort to ensure that your product wins the highest NHTSA rating on every metric.

Further Thoughts on Managing Risk and Uncertainty

Today's most successful companies are operating in a market environment of constant change—and therefore must manage risk and uncertainty in an objective and proactive way.

There's often very little data available to know what the future might hold. However, if you identify the things you *do* know—and if you explicitly recognize and manage factors you can control—you can dramatically improve your chance of success. When you anticipate what might happen, you can prepare for the possibilities. You're able to start putting pieces in place that allow you to take fast, appropriate action when needed. This preparation can provide a huge strategic advantage when change occurs. You can act quickly, while competitors are caught unprepared.

Using Scenario Analysis

Being agile means acting quickly when an opportunity presents itself—which requires alignment among members of a management team. However, there is often no time for in-depth discussion and debate when the need to act is urgent.

This is why resilient and flexible companies discuss and debate potential strategies *before* unfolding events demand urgent action. Scenario analysis is one valuable tool for stimulating such conversations and that allows managers to mentally rehearse their potential response to future events. Teams who have talked frankly about scenarios that might unfold in the future can interpret events more rationally when they *do* occur. They have already hashed out their differences and even covered the pros and cons of potential responses.

Let's say you're a university considering how to compete in online learning. You may have already incorporated this approach somewhat into certain classes as a supplement to classroom activity; perhaps you even offer noncredit courses for free (as Stanford, MIT, and others do). However, you're beginning to foresee the day when you will offer online courses, or even entire online degree programs, for credit. You don't know how fast this transition might occur, how much you will be able to charge for the courses, or how you would manage such things as admissions, group assignments, grades, and identity authentication (that is, proving that the student taking the test is who she claims to be). You wonder what programs you should be investing in, how much, and when to invest.

The following are some steps you could take to gain understanding of the uncertain future in the higher education market.

Step One: Outline the Parameters of Change

The first step in scenario analysis is to outline the parameters that define future scenarios. In the university example, these might include the following:

- **Regulatory.** What new regulations might be instituted to govern how schools conduct online courses, award course credit and degrees, and whether or not students can use federal loan funds to pay for these courses?
- **Societal.** Will employers accept degrees earned entirely online as equivalent to on-campus degrees? Should admissions standards change, given that online delivery will effectively expand each university's capacity? How will online offerings help, or hurt, the university's brand and prestige, or affect alumni giving?
- **Demand.** How many people in the United States and other countries are interested in paying for online courses, and how much will they be willing to pay? Which courses and degrees will be most popular? How many students can a given course or degree accommodate? Will geography matter at all when choosing an online university?
- **Technological.** What technologies will be developed for recording and accessing lectures, assessing student performance, managing group projects, authenticating identities, and interacting with students one-on-one? How will students interact with each other in the future? Which companies will offer these technologies, and how will they charge for using them? Which technologies will become standard, and which will become obsolete?
- **Competitive.** What courses and degrees will other universities offer online? How will requirements, grading, and the student experience be different for online versus on-campus programs? What new business models will be developed for offering online courses?

Step Two: Identify Potential Future Scenarios

The second step is to describe and name a set of scenarios that could transpire. These can be derived from combinations of the parameters laid out in step one.

Peter Schwartz, author of *The Art of the Long View*, suggests that you should develop no fewer than four scenarios and should name each one. The name provides an easy handle for discussing a complex set of outcomes, facilitating discussion and dialogue.

Schwartz suggests that companies define one scenario called the "Official Future." This, he says, is the "set of implicit assumptions behind most institutional policies"—assumptions to which people subscribe almost unconsciously. According to Schwartz, the Official Future is often more a product of propaganda and wishful thinking than of objectivity.

Many companies' Official Futures go something like this: "We will continue to grow and protect the capabilities that allow us to deliver our current product offerings. Customers will continue to value our offerings, and competitors will continue to compete much as they do now." It's simply hard to imagine that things won't continue much the same as they have. Flushing out the organization's version of the Official Future enables managers to assess it objectively and to decide how likely or unlikely—and even how desirable or undesirable—it is.

Schwartz suggests another useful scenario name: "My Worst Nightmare." This encourages leaders to talk openly together about subjects they often avoid. Verbalizing the elements of the My Worst Nightmare scenario helps them mentally rehearse how they might respond should aspects of the scenario begin to play out one day. This rehearsal also mitigates the paralysis and fear that may occur when some of these events actually begin to transpire.

Other scenarios comprise "packages" of outcomes, using the parameters the team has described. For example, scenarios for the university example might include

- **The Winners and Losers Scenario.** A small set of universities invests heavily in online course content and differentiated technology. These universities capture a large share of the market and continue to gain greater and greater revenues and prestige—while other universities that failed to seize this opportunity shrink in size, stature, and financial success.
- **The Everyone and Everything Scenario.** Extremely easy-to-use, low-cost technologies and industry-standard processes are developed, allowing any college to implement online courses with great ease. Online degrees become as valued by employers as degrees earned on-campus. Students accept remote learning as an attractive alternative to the on-campus experience, even at top-tier universities. Every college contains a mix of online and on-campus students who collaborate seamlessly.
- **The Specialist Scenario.** Certain degrees are proven to be more adaptable to an online delivery mechanism. For example, technical degrees become predominantly delivered online, while liberal arts courses remain predominantly in an on-campus format. Because schools can economically deliver online content to many students simultaneously, colleges become more and more specialized, focusing on highly specific degree programs and awarding those specialized degrees to more and more students.

John Morrow, senior director of operations at Cisco, has used scenario analysis very effectively at several points in his career. He explains that its purpose is not to describe *every* scenario that may occur, and that it's in fact impossible to do so given the number of parameters at play. The important thing is for the management team to recognize differences in their assumptions about what is most likely to happen, and to illuminate the range of outcomes that might occur. When managers practice thinking about the possibilities, they can make decisions more effectively once events begin to play out.

Step Three: Decide What Actions to Take Based on the Scenarios That Might Transpire

The final step is for the team to discuss the scenarios and decide what action to take and what metrics and events to monitor.

"The payoff for identifying and discussing potential future scenarios," Morrow suggests, "is distilling the 'so whats'"—that is, answering questions such as:

- What should we do if we have to compete in the world described in Scenario A? What about Scenario B, or C?
- What actions should we take *no matter what* scenario unfolds?
- What investments should we make to protect us from the downside of each potential scenario?
- What investments should we make to enable us to take advantage of each scenario's potential upside?
- What metrics and events should we monitor to glean clues about how the future might unfold?

Morrow points out that managers act in accordance with their own view of the future world—a view that varies greatly from one manager to the next: "When key leaders hold different assumptions about what [might occur], they can't act in a coordinated way, especially when they face unexpected market events." Shining a light on these differences is key to developing alignment and adapting together as market changes unfold.

"There are future benefits to scenario thinking," Morrow explains, "but there is also a tremendous real-time benefit. A well-designed conversation about scenarios is inherently collaborative and constructive. It either affirms alignment or exposes misalignment. People show up in different ways in these conversations. Some are obstructionists, some are stuck in the past, and some engage in undisciplined thinking. Gaining an understanding of team members' thinking, and *why* these beliefs and assumptions differ, is very valuable in both the here and now and the future."

Recognize, Manage, and Test the Assumptions Required to Succeed

Even when you are implementing a relatively straightforward business initiative, it pays to understand clearly what assumptions must hold true for you to be successful, and to take deliberate steps to manage these assumptions.

Any sound strategic choice rests on a set of beliefs about what your customers want, what you are capable of, and what competitors will do. Your job is to document these beliefs explicitly so that you can continuously validate that they still hold true. If it becomes clear that they do not, you might need to make a change in strategy.

I often observe companies that cling to failing strategies long after they should abandon them. They've forgotten why they pursued them in the first place, and do not realize—or at least admit—that the circumstances that led them to choose the strategy no longer apply. For example, a company that I know of employed a highly skilled, lavishly compensated sales force when it first set out to penetrate a new market, then later failed to realize, once it gained dominant market share, that the high-cost sales force had become an expensive liability.

Let's say you were thinking of expanding into a new geographic market. You would seek out data on the market size and on pricing, and speak with potential customers to understand their needs. You would assess the local competition to understand their capabilities, strengths, and weaknesses. You would decide how many salespeople would be required to penetrate the market. To justify the investment, you would develop financial projections. In preparing these projections, you should ask yourself:

- What assumptions must hold true for this initiative to succeed?
- Which assumptions can we control—at least partially?
  - o At what milestone in our process could we test these assumptions?

o   Can we put metrics in place to monitor trends in these assumptions?

o   Who will be responsible for managing these assumptions to maximize our chance of success?

- Which assumptions are outside our control?

o   How will we measure trends related to these uncontrollable assumptions?

o   Who will be responsible for monitoring these metrics?

o   What "trigger points" regarding these metrics would indicate that we need to consider a change in strategy?

The example in Table 7.3 shows one company's key assumptions in entering a country where it had no prior experience, and how it set out to test and manage these assumptions.

As you can see, this company laid out its assumptions clearly, and assigned dates and responsibilities for validating each one. The management team identified specific events that would trigger a change in strategy—such as failure to get government approval for the new plant or inability to achieve 5 percent share in one specific geographic region within six months.

As the months pass, this organization will gain more and better information about the market and about its capabilities to serve it effectively. If customers, competitors, costs, and other factors are not as anticipated, leadership can make the necessary adjustments.

In Conclusion

We have seen how all business leaders must anticipate and deal with uncertainty. Making quick decisions in ambiguous environments while managing risks related to demand, competition, and the development of new capabilities is an essential skill for anyone leading an organization nowadays.

In my years of experience working with companies in every industry, I have seen companies consistently make three mistakes in managing risk and uncertainty: **taking no action, engaging in**

Table 7.3 Example: Market-Entry Strategy Assumptions

Assumptions	Controllable or Uncontrollable?	How Might We Test This?	Who Is Responsible, and by When
This country market consumes $100 million in our product category each year.	Uncontrollable in the short term	Get data from trade association. Validate with customer interviews.	Smith – December 15
We can gain government approval to establish a plant on a leased site.	Partially controllable	Meet with government officials to conduct preliminary review of documentation. If denied, reconsider whether market entry is viable.	Forsythe – January 20
The cost of producing our product in this market will be equal to the cost in the United States.	Partially controllable	Get quotes from raw material suppliers; assess labor costs and shipping costs.	James – February 28
We can hire and train five local salespeople within six months.	Controllable	Engage a recruiter to identify candidates. Assess level of talent and what salaries will be required to attract qualified individuals.	Liu – March 15
We can achieve 10% market share in two years, with margins similar to what we earn in the United States.	Controllable	Focus initially on one geographic region and one segment of the market. If we can achieve 5% market share within six months in that small focus area, while holding price on par with U.S. levels, we have a good shot at reaching 10% share within two years. If not, consider exiting the market or revising market entry strategy.	Chen – June 15 (interim update on March 15)

me-tooism, and **being overconfident.** Avoiding these mistakes should be Job 1 of every leader.

As you deal with uncertainty in your own business, industry, markets, and regulatory environment, consider applying the following principles to manage risks:

- **Design your strategy to maximize learning.** When moving into risky strategic territory, think about what initial steps would enable you to understand what you need to learn to succeed. Then design your strategy to meet these learning objectives.

- **Manage technology risk.** Ask yourself what objectives you could potentially achieve through technology advancement. What risks do these new technologies present? What development and learning will be required to employ them?

- **Manage customer-demand risk.** Identify and set out to directly address consumer concerns that might stop customers from buying.

- **Think from the ground up to develop a differentiated offering.** Ask yourself in what arenas your thinking has become constrained by established practices, beliefs, and norms. If you were to reduce your problem to its fundamental truths, what new and different solutions might your company produce?

- **Be the best at something.** Define the target customer group your product or service will be ideally suited for, and the ways this group will regard yours as the very best available solution.

- **Employ scenario analysis.** Discuss and debate potential scenarios and strategies for succeeding in them, *before* such events demand urgent action. Teams that have talked frankly about scenarios that might unfold can interpret events more rationally when they *do* occur.

- **Recognize, manage, and test the assumptions required to succeed.** Understand clearly what assumptions must hold true for you to be successful with any strategic initiative, and take deliberate steps to manage these assumptions.

Chapter Eight

Turning a Strategic Corner

Take the First Steps, Shed What Doesn't Fit, Experiment, and Reinforce

L ike every other company in the cellular handset market, Samsung was blindsided by the 2007 introduction of the then-revolutionary Apple iPhone. But while Nokia and Black-Berry both precipitously lost market share as the iPhone took their place, Samsung emerged strong—capturing a highly profitable 40 percent of worldwide market share by 2012, compared to 13 percent for Apple.

With about the same annual revenues ($190 billion) as Microsoft, Google, Amazon, and Facebook combined, Samsung Electronics currently dominates nearly every product category in which it competes. Now, facing declining profits from hardware sales and having set a goal of doubling corporate sales over the next six years,[1] Samsung chairman Lee Kun-hee has concluded that the only avenue for substantial future growth is to create *entirely new product categories*—and to become more competitive in software, content, and services. The trouble is that Samsung has not historically excelled in these areas. And although its vertically integrated structure and its speed, discipline, and efficiency make it a superb fast-follower, creativity and innovation are not Samsung's areas of strength.

How can a company that has spent years honing its ability to quickly copy and improve its competitors' products turn the corner to become more creative and innovative—to the point where it can invent the entirely new trends and product categories that it needs to drive growth?

As he did two decades ago when he met with dozens of his executives and issued the now legendary order to "Change everything but your wife and children," Lee is again calling for transformation. He's seen that companies can be at the top of the mobile handset business one year and at the bottom the next. And it's not just Nokia and BlackBerry—Motorola, Ericsson, and HTC have all enjoyed time at the summit, only to fall out of favor and to see their market share plummet. Change will be *essential* to stay at the top.

Samsung's risk is high at this point. Its smartphones share the Android platform with many other manufacturers, including Chinese suppliers like Xiaomi, which builds phones that cost hundreds of dollars less than Samsung's popular Galaxy S4 model. Consumers who like and are accustomed to the Android platform can easily switch to a lower-priced phone the next time they are ready for an upgrade—leaving Samsung in a vulnerable position. The company wants to differentiate its user experience from lower-cost competitors, and to reduce its reliance on the Android platform by partnering with Intel and others to help make its new Linux-based operating system, Tizen, successful.

In a company-wide email in June 2013, Lee stated: "As we move forward, we must resist complacency and thoughts of being good enough, as these will prevent us from becoming better … We must create an environment of ingenuity, where autonomy and creativity abound."[2]

Much remains to be seen concerning how Samsung will gain the capabilities to become a leader in creating new product concepts, trends, and categories. The company has taken some initial steps, such as establishing open innovation centers and accelerator programs in New York and California. These groups will search for start-ups to partner with, invest in, or acquire. Start-ups accepted into the accelerator program will receive full Samsung benefits, legal resources, and insight into Samsung's product road maps.

Lee has made his intention clear to employees: become more innovative, develop differentiated software, and create new product categories—including content and services—for Samsung to dominate. He cannot, however, spell out every detail of Samsung's future journey. The company and its people will have to learn along the way.

When Jim Collins set out to write *Good to Great*, he expected leaders of the eleven successful companies his team profiled—Kimberly-Clark, Kroger, Walgreens, and Wells Fargo, among others—to cite *gaining alignment and commitment* as critical to turning the corner to achieve success. However, his research team discovered that leaders didn't stress the importance of these steps. The successful companies *did*, however, need to understand their "hedgehog" concept—that is, what they could be the best in the world at, which would ignite their passion and drive their economic engine. But there was never a "miracle moment" when the companies announced their transformation. Rather, Collins explains, it was "a quiet, deliberate process of figuring out what needed to be done to create the best future results, and then simply taking those steps, one after another."[3] In other words—these "good-to-great" companies worked continuously and iteratively to improve, and let their early successes build momentum. Although they may have appeared to be overnight successes to observers, people within the companies knew that such change—and growth—could only come a little at a time.

I worked for Kimberly-Clark during the transformational period that Collins studied, as it shifted from being a paper company to being a consumer products company. During this period, the company generated cumulative stock returns 4.1 times the general market, beating rival P&G and outperforming Coca-Cola, 3M, and General Electric. As employees during this period, we didn't talk about "transformation," but we did talk—a lot—about continuous improvement. We talked about improving safety, cost, and quality, and innovating to keep babies drier and happier in the disposable diapers we designed and manufactured. It was pretty simple, and it felt good.

This chapter will explore the cycle of change that companies undergo, depicted in Figure 8.1. As you might conclude from studying the figure, you can start this process at any point in the cycle.

The Setili Cycle of Change is an iterative process. Although each step builds on the other, you don't need to complete one step before starting the next, and you don't need to take the steps in a particular order. Likely as not, you'll be doing parts of each step simultaneously.

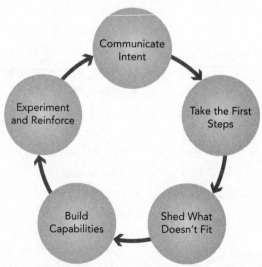

Figure 8.1 Turning a Strategic Corner: The Setili Cycle of Change

Communicate Intent

Although it doesn't have to be the first, an important step in executing any change in strategic direction is simply communicating the intent. Lee Kun-hee did so by making it clear that he intends Samsung to become an innovation leader. He doesn't know exactly how the company will accomplish this; fortunately, he doesn't have to know for the company to succeed.

Communicate Intent to Employees

Especially when fast change is needed—which it usually is—no leadership team can know or predict all the steps that will be required. It is impossible to tell everyone what to do. And even if you did have the time and ability to explain what each function and level should do to execute change, you wouldn't *want* to—because conditions would have evolved by the time you spelled things out, making your instructions obsolete. Being too specific about actions can be counterproductive, and can hinder adaptability and agility.

Therefore, communicate the *intent* of the change—the desired future state—in clear and compelling language early in the process, allowing others to figure out their *own* way to contribute. When they know what the organization is seeking, employees from the top of your organization to the bottom—in geographies you don't often visit, and in every function—can apply their own ingenuity to help bring about the desired future state. Employees make many decisions each day. When they know your intent, they can make right decisions that will have everyone heading in a common direction.

Figure 8.2 depicts how lack of clear intent—shown on the left—leads to slow progress. Geoffrey Moore, author of *Dealing with Darwin* and *Crossing the Chasm*, would say that it leads to *zero* progress—which is often the case.

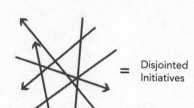 = Disjointed Initiatives    = Strategic Alignment

Figure 8.2 Unclear Versus Clear Intent

On the right, you can see what happens when the intent is clear. Because it's easier to go *with* the flow than against it, people naturally follow this path. Once they know which way the river is ultimately running, they fall in step—because it's fun. If you've ever been in a marching band, you know how exhilarating stepping in time with others can be—the cadence of the drums is thrilling, and it feels good to be part of something bigger than yourself. Your employees can feel this too, when the intent is clear and they are given the autonomy to work together to get there.

Communicate Intent to Suppliers, Partners, and Customers

Sharing your intent with suppliers and partners is at least as important as sharing it with employees. After all, your staff is with you day in and day out, so you can guide their efforts daily. But suppliers and partners speak with you less frequently, so clearly expressing your company's intended direction can be hugely useful in allowing them to intelligently align their efforts with your intent. If they know where you are headed, they can gear their investments, systems, and innovations to help you on your journey. Similarly, you should share your intent with customers, so that they can prepare their organizations for the changes that may come down the road and guide you about how their needs are likely to evolve and either mesh or clash with your vision.

Glenn Lurie, AT&T's president for emerging enterprises and partnerships, negotiated AT&T's exclusive iPhone and iPad deals with Apple when those products were introduced. Lurie foresaw that for the iPhone to be successful, AT&T—a company with more than 250,000 employees—had to challenge BAU (business as usual). This meant giving Apple control over areas AT&T had not let OEMs control in the past, like the user interface, establishing a brand-new activation process, and more. According to Lurie, "The one thing we learned is that changing BAU … is really hard. My team had to drive a message throughout the organization that 'we are going to change *everything* to make this a success.'"[4]

"The number one thing is relationships," says Lurie. In his view, building a trusted partnership is equally as important as trying to win the best deal for AT&T. "When we first began talking with Apple, we had to work to establish a trusted relationship. Ultimately, AT&T and Apple achieved the kind of partnership where we could disagree, work through the problems, and walk out on the same page and smiling. In the end, I believe we changed the industry."[5]

Building a flexible partnership with Apple and shaking things up within AT&T paid off, as AT&T benefited from being the exclusive provider of the iPhone for three years and iPad for one year. During this time, AT&T Wireless gained 170 basis points of profit margin and came from behind to surpass Verizon Wireless revenues.

Lurie now is at the center of an explosion of new technologies associated with what AT&T calls Connected Devices—sometimes called the Internet of Things, the Internet of Everything, or machine-to-machine communication. Because growth in AT&T's traditional wireless phone business has slowed in recent years, the company has identified this market—wirelessly connecting anything and everything—as crucial for company growth.

AT&T's strategic push to connect myriad nonphone devices ranges from security and navigation systems, to sensors that measure soil moisture and chemical levels for automated control of farms, to devices for monitoring aircraft engines, power grids, and industrial equipment, to devices that analyze an individual's health or athletic performance and transmit the results wirelessly to his or her doctor or coach. *Wall Street Journal* technology columnist Walt Mossberg once said that Lurie had "one of the most interesting jobs in the mobile industry."[6]

There's no doubt that this market presents huge potential for growth. Cisco estimates that the number of devices connected to the Internet will rise from about ten billion today to fifty billion by 2020;[7] Gartner Inc. predicts that the Internet of Things will add $1.9 trillion to the global economy by 2020.[8] Of course, there is also great uncertainty—given that most of the products that will fuel this projected growth haven't even been invented yet.

Now, as Lurie leads the charge to create a leadership position for AT&T in the Internet of Things, his goal is to build platforms that "can help make the partner's life easier, which then makes the user experience better."[9] To that end, Lurie's team is forming partnerships with numerous small start-ups that have developed great ideas and approaches for making life easier, more efficient, and healthier. But they're also joining forces with behemoths such as GM and GE that want to transform their industries. In this environment of uncertainty, Lurie says, "You've got to remain flexible, because neither partner knows what will happen down the road."[10]

AT&T—like Cisco, Intel, GE, GM, and other companies that are making huge strategic investments in the Internet of Things—knows the market will be big. Yet it cannot predict what form it will take or who the winners will be. Each of these companies is placing a big bet and turning a major strategic corner. They're all part of a complex, intertwined ecosystem of suppliers, partners, and customers. Often the companies they deal with play more than one role; Microsoft, for instance, is both a partner and a competitor to Cisco. Communicating the intent to these other players—while staying flexible to adapt along the way—is crucial to making strategic progress.

Take the First Steps

As Clay Christensen and his coauthors say in their book *Seeing What's Next: Using Theories of Innovation to Predict Industry Change*, "data becomes conclusive only when it's too late to take action based on its conclusions."[11] This means that you will often need to take action before you feel fully ready, especially if there is a chance that the competition could preempt you. Sometimes you just need to take the first steps, and figure the rest out as you go.

As we discussed in chapter 7, strategic initiatives are always based on *assumptions*. You can't know everything when you begin—but you *can* have a clear plan for testing and managing the assumptions and for learning. When Frank Blake took the reins of Home Depot in 2007, the company's share price growth was lagging behind both its primary competitor, Lowe's, and the market as a whole. Lowe's was beating Home Depot on comparable store sales growth quarter after quarter, and the downturn in the housing market was just beginning.

Blake looked outside the home improvement industry to examine what companies like McDonald's, Continental Airlines, PetSmart, and Staples were doing. Some were innovating new retail approaches—but some, like McDonald's, were gaining competitive ground simply by getting back to the basics of good service, clean restrooms, and good food.

In the end, Blake and his team made very simple but profoundly effective changes. For example, customer research showed that store associate availability was a problem, and that Home Depot had strayed far from the skilled service model on which Bernie Marcus and Arthur Blank founded the company. So one of the first things Blake did upon taking over as CEO was to increase the number of associates working in each store.

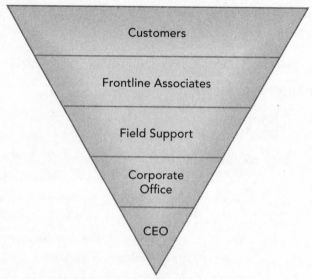

Figure 8.3 The Home Depot Inverted Triangle

He dusted off the "inverted triangle" shown in Figure 8.3 to reignite the philosophy that the founders had established: "If you take care of the associates, they will take care of the customers, and everything else takes care of itself." The role of the corporate office is to "absorb the complexity" of the field, serve the store associates, and keep things simple for the stores so that they can focus on serving customers. The role of the CEO—at the bottom—is simply to support the others. The triangle fit perfectly with Blake's low-key, humble style.

Blake explained the first steps that Home Depot needed to take, in a single-page document simply named "Home Depot's Five Key Priorities." Each of the five priorities had four or five immediate steps to support it. Even now, seven years later, managers display the framed list—touting Home Depot's five key priorities—in their offices:[12]

- Associate engagement
- Product excitement

- Product availability
- Shopping environment
- Own the pro

The approach worked. By pursuing the five priorities Blake laid out in 2007, Home Depot dramatically improved its performance. In 2012, the company recorded a robust growth in sales of 6.2 percent for the full year, whereas Lowe's was just 2.2 percent for the full year.

Let's look at just a few examples of the transformation that helped vault Home Depot ahead of its competition:

Logistics investments, leading to improved customer service. When Blake became CEO, suppliers delivered 75 percent of product direct to the store—which meant that store associates didn't have time to serve customers because they were busy stocking the shelves. Yet the process was not effective: "out of stocks" were one of the customers' biggest complaints in 2007. Now, thanks to supply chain investments, suppliers deliver only 25 percent of product directly to stores. The rest is delivered through Home Depot's own distribution centers. The trucks are packed in a way that allows employees to optimally unload product—from the front to the back of the store. This approach maximizes the speed and efficiency with which store associates can stock the shelves, and minimizes disruption in the aisles. Whereas store associates used to spend 40 percent of their time with customers and 60 percent performing other tasks, it's now the opposite—60 percent of their time is spent with customers. This transformation required a multiyear investment in distribution centers, systems, and training, but it paid off in a better customer experience.

Interconnected retail. Home Depot's performance in interconnected or *omnichannel* retailing is also impressive. Almost one out of every three online orders is completed in the store, either through Buy Online Pick Up In Store or Buy Online Ship to Store. These systems benefit both the customer and Home Depot; the customer can count on the product being ready to pick up when he or she arrives, and Home Depot enjoys increased sales, as one out of every five customers who come to the store to pick up or return a product bought online purchases additional items while there.

Home Depot also uses technology to enhance the in-store experience. For example, a customer can speak the name of a product into the voice search feature, and the Home Depot app will lead him or her to its location in the store. Store employees can help a customer select a product from the "endless aisle" of four hundred thousand SKUs offered online, versus the forty thousand in the store. In this way, the online experience leads customers to the stores, and the in-store experience leads customers online.

Technologies to enhance the "pro" customers' businesses. Although Home Depot's "pros"—painters, contractors, plumbers, and the like—make up only 3 percent of customers, they comprise more than 35 percent of the company's sales. Market research revealed that hassle-free returns and detailed receipts are among the top satisfaction drivers for pros, so Home Depot invested in robust technology to help these individuals manage their businesses. Now, pros get electronic receipts and can track purchases made on multiple credit cards by multiple employees on multiple jobs. They can export the data right into their accounting systems and create estimates for their customers with real-time pricing and product images.

Blake was clear about his intent, moved immediately to take the first steps, and invested in a continuous and coordinated way over a period of years to shape Home Depot's culture and capability. The results have been impressive.

Analysts at Janney Capital Markets stated that Blake "makes running one of the five largest retailers in the country seem easy—[even] smooth. It's not easy. It has been a dramatic turnaround, one in which HD has gone from a market share loser to a market share gainer . . . in which a company [that] senselessly wasted capital at times [is] now a capital efficient machine . . . that generates cash, buys back stock, and continues to recapture customers lost due to shoddy service almost a decade ago."[13]

Shed What Doesn't Fit

Strategic change requires that you eliminate the parts of your business that don't fit the new direction. Yet companies often fail to do this, because they are in love with the products, people, ideas, and capabilities that built their success. They continue to pour resources into mediocre or failing product lines, even when they'd be better off spending the money elsewhere. They hang on to distracting and underperforming business units, long after they should have fixed or divested those units.

Occasionally, companies are bound by contracts, partnerships, assets, and liabilities that limit their ability to make changes. However, you can usually overcome these restrictions with just a bit of creativity. When you shed unneeded pieces of your business, you can both redeploy resources to more important priorities and free up management attention to focus on moving toward your intended future.

Consider the following as you review your own company for things to purge:

- **Product lines, brands, and technologies.** Ford closed its Mercury line; sold Jaguar Cars, Land Rover, and Hertz Rent-a-Car; and closed fourteen plants.[14]
- **Assets**. Southwest sold eighty-eight Boeing 717 aircraft—which it acquired in the AirTran merger—to Delta Air Lines in order to maintain its traditional focus and efficiency by flying only Boeing 737s.[15]

- **Leaders, staff, and organizational capabilities.** For example, removing leaders who do not fit your intended culture can be critical to success. Many companies also outsource functions they deem to be nonstrategic, such as manufacturing and call centers.
- **Customers and market segments.** For example, you might exit certain geographies—such as when Google conducted a partial exit from China in 2010 due to government censorship of its search results—or leave your least profitable market segments.
- **Partnerships, suppliers, and channels.** For example, some companies choose to end relationships with distributors and instead sell direct to customers; others end relationships with suppliers who are not aligned with their future vision.
- **Outdated values, beliefs, and ways of working.** Shedding elements of your culture that don't fit with the direction you wish to head is difficult but crucial. For example, Lou Gerstner, former CEO of IBM, wished to end "obsessive perfectionism" and "studying things to death," so he began to reward employees for getting things done fast.[16]

Robert Nardelli, who was Frank Blake's predecessor as CEO of Home Depot, had distracted management from the core retail business by investing heavily in growing a distribution business that catered to the construction industry. He deployed much of the best talent in the company to the distribution side of the business because that's where the growth was. Blake reversed this trend by divesting the distribution business and refocusing Home Depot's management team 100 percent on improving the store experience for customers.

Within your new, streamlined organization, consider changes in organizational structure and processes to speed decision making, cultivate innovation, increase accountability, and improve efficiency and effectiveness. You will often find the shortest path to these outcomes when you start shedding what no longer fits.

Build New Capabilities

It's a mistake to restrict strategic choices to what you can achieve with today's capabilities. When heading in a new strategic direction, consider what competencies you'll need to reach your goals—then create a plan to acquire those capabilities.

Capabilities include not just skills and knowledge but also technologies, business processes, manufacturing, sales, service, and more. You can gain each of these capabilities in a variety of different ways—through acquisitions, technology investments, training, recruiting, and developmental career progressions.

When Steve Macadam joined industrial products manufacturer EnPro Industries as CEO in 2008, he noticed that highly effective practices that had been developed within one division of the company rarely made their way into sister divisions. Conversations between divisions occurred regularly at the level of the division presidents, but not at the middle and lower levels in the organization—the very places where many decisions were being made and much work was being completed. Hierarchy was an entrenched part of the culture, so it was almost unheard of for one division to pitch in to help another.

EnPro manufactures seals, bearings, engines, and other proprietary products for critical applications, such as nuclear power plants, aerospace, oil and gas, and defense. Therefore, innovation, quality, and technical excellence are vital. Macadam and his team knew that they would need to establish a new way of working to maintain robust growth.

They were aware that their organization could be more agile and adaptive if each employee *owned his or her own work*—if he or she pursued opportunities and made decisions without having to wait for the boss's instructions or approval. They also wanted to build greater connections between the divisions without adding central control that would slow the organization down and impede flexibility.

The team worked for several months to articulate the new "dual bottom line" culture they wished to create. In addition to creating superior financial performance, they sought to enable within EnPro the "full release of human possibility," captured in the following six principles:

- **Personal vision and inspiration.** Understanding one's vision, purpose, identity, or destiny provides the inspiration for growth and development.
- **Empowerment to create.** People and workgroups need to be "their own boss"; each individual should be empowered to influence and create his current situation and future, while accepting the responsibility to maintain a high standard of excellence.
- **Growth and learning.** Each individual should be eager and hungry to learn, grow, and develop, and help others do the same.
- **Freedom.** Each employee has the authority and discretion to pursue what she cares about, to be creative, and imagine new ideas to which she is emotionally committed. She should be willing to take informed risks, while accepting accountability for the good of the enterprise.
- **Connection.** Each employee should each act as a whole-hearted individual—authentic, vulnerable, and eager to listen. We should act with deep mutual respect and caring for others, and create networks to share learnings across our organization.
- **Commitment of full self.** Each individual should feel confident and secure in delivering all of his gifts through individual initiative. We should believe in the best of others while delivering excellence in ourselves.

To aid in achieving this organizational transformation, EnPro established a set of "councils" that brought together strong upper- and midlevel leaders from all divisions to improve practices and performance in strategy, innovation, human development, sales and marketing, manufacturing, and finance. Employees who participated were expected to allocate a full 50 percent of their time to the councils. Having some of their most talented employees give up so much time was of course difficult for the divisions—but the investment is paying off.

Through their work on the councils, employees learned how to collaborate effectively as peers when no one was in charge. They worked with employees from outside their divisions and came to feel very connected and committed, not only to their division but to the corporation as a whole. They learned to play for the EnPro team.

The councils stimulated the flow of ideas, improved the speed with which new initiatives progress, and spurred collaboration between the divisions—leading to better decision making and learning. Employees who embark on a new project now have a network of colleagues, spread through multiple divisions, to bounce ideas off of. The entire organization's capability—not just that of the employees who participated—has grown as a result. As Macadam describes it, players both "pitch" ideas and approaches to their own and other divisions, and "catch" ideas by implementing them in their own divisions.

EnPro also embarked on a series of powerful experiential learning programs to nurture this change in its culture. Every employee across North and South America, Europe, and Asia participated in at least two full days of training to better understand his or her role and obligation in making decisions. They all also received training in self-awareness and in how to resolve differences.

The change was profound. Employees came to understand both their freedom and responsibility to innovate and contribute to overall company performance—and the results were apparent. Employees on one manufacturing line reduced waste by 30 percent; another group of plant workers designed an important breakthrough product in only eight weeks; a third redesigned their entire production line, thereby reducing by 40 percent the time required to make an engine. EnPro employees have established new and better processes across a wide range of disciplines—pricing, sales-force effectiveness, manufacturing efficiency, delivery performance, and more—all specifically focused on supporting EnPro's strategic objectives.

As one plant floor employee explained, "I've worked here for twenty years and have never been treated this way. People respect us and appreciate what we are doing. We can get things done that we couldn't before." Many employees remarked that the training had helped them in their personal as well as work lives.

"People like to do what they are capable of doing, under their own guidance," says Macadam. "When work teams have an idea of how to improve something, they no longer have to ask for permission; they just do it. They can execute changes on their own. The supervisor's role has shifted to being coach and supporter. When employees see something they'd like to change, they put their supervisors to work—asking them for help to get what's needed to make the improvements."

While this shift in culture has improved EnPro's organizational capability, employees benefit as well from having greater control over their own work and business decisions. They've gained greater visibility to customers and to teams at other sites, and now have access to more career advancement options. One plant floor worker progressed to a process engineering role, something that would not have happened prior to EnPro's cultural transformation.

EnPro invested in building a new culture to become more self-sustaining and agile, and a better place to work—a place where people could realize their full potential for professional creativity, innovation, and fulfillment. Its investment in building culture, capabilities, and community has paid off in new, differentiated products; higher productivity; and superior market responsiveness.

The following are some ways to build new capabilities in your own organization:

- Recruit employees who have the capabilities and values that you would like the entire organization to shift toward, and who will be passionately committed to making your vision a reality—while accepting both the triumphs and setbacks in getting there.
- Choose investors, suppliers, technology partners, and channel partners that can fill capability gaps or that can help you build internal capabilities.
- Attract customers from whom you can learn, and engage them in the process.
- Choose the right organizational structure to meet your capability goals. For example, some companies have gained speed and agility by forming partially autonomous "start-ups" *within* the larger organization.
- Prepare for the inevitable friction that may occur as your organization transitions from one set of capabilities and values to another. Communicate transparently about the transition, and provide a path for employees to acquire the new skills to succeed.
- Choose the right people and build the right culture for agility. For example, Delta Air Lines and AT&T both look to hire courageous, flexible people for their most forward-reaching business units.

Experiment and Reinforce

A critical stage in implementing strategic change is experimenting and learning, then replicating or reinforcing what works best. Today's most agile companies make a deliberate effort to accept a certain degree of failure as a part of that process.

Seek Change and Welcome Failures

A couple of years ago, my husband and I decided to learn to play ice hockey. One of the first drills the coach prescribed was the "Superman" drill. We skated fast, then threw ourselves down on the ice, flying face-first, belly-down across the ice, Superman-style. The purpose was to practice recovery from falls and getting back up on your feet and skating again as quickly as possible. It was fun, if absurd looking, and a huge confidence builder. We learned not to let falls slow us down.

Organizations can get bogged down and lose their passion and adrenaline when employees begin to fear "falling"—and therefore avoid change and failure. Thomas Watson Sr. served as CEO of IBM from 1914 to 1956 and said, "The fastest way to succeed is to double your rate of failure." Failure can be a *good* sign of company growth; it shows that you are trying lots of things.

I met Intercontinental Exchange CEO Jeffrey Sprecher in December 2012, just two days before he announced that his company was going to buy the New York Stock Exchange. Sprecher had decided early in his life that even though people tend not to like change, our lives are defined by moments of change. He explains that despite our general tendency to avoid it, "Change is one of the best things for you, and I've always pushed toward change. [It] inevitably means mistakes; so if you make a mistake and things go poorly, don't act like they are going well. Recognize the mistake, and change course."[17]

The story of how Sprecher started from scratch by buying electrical generating plants, then creating Intercontinental Exchange from scratch, and then buying the NYSE, sounds rather haphazard and opportunistic—but what he did worked. He sought change, dealt objectively and quickly with failure, and *kept moving*.

Agile companies accept failure as a part of learning and recognize the opportunity inherent in change. They reinforce these attitudes among their leaders and employees at every level.

Conduct Experiments

Countless action-oriented leaders have lamented the fact that their corporations take too long to make decisions and tend to be highly averse to risk. Especially if investment decisions are tied to an annual budgeting cycle, opportunities often pass companies by before they are able to decide and to take any action.

Agile companies take small but immediate steps to test the waters before making big, risky course changes. They run experiments, such as pilot programs. This is particularly advisable when making revolutionary innovations, because it's often impossible to tell in these cases how customers will respond. If customers have never seen or even imagined the new product you are offering, they cannot tell you whether or not they will buy it. Therefore, it's often necessary to simply "try more things," to experiment and tinker to figure out how the customer will use the innovation and whether or not he or she will find it valuable.

Businesses such as software, e-commerce, and online services can learn the results of such experiments within hours. Facebook runs hundreds of different versions of its site at any given time. You may see a version of an ad with one set of colors and features, and I see another—simultaneously. Facebook engineers measure customer response, and retain the versions that perform the best, eliminating the others. Etsy, Netflix, Amazon, Twitter, and Google similarly apply this process, called DevOps (a fusion of development and operations), to improve not just customer response but their site's reliability and security.[18] Each incremental alteration to the user experience is minor, so users can adapt gradually to change. This rapid innovation and learning cycle has led these companies' success.

Of course, not every industry has the rapid development cycle of cloud-based software systems like Facebook. Changes to aircraft designs are years in the making—yet experimentation is still important here. Delta Air Lines executives work side-by-side with flight attendants to test new cabin configurations that are under consideration. A top Delta leader remarked, "We took out the back galley to make room for two additional rows of seats. We love the new revenue, but had no place to store the trash—I had to work a flight as a flight attendant to realize this. We developed a workaround, and had time to prepare crew for the changes they would need to make in beverage service."

Whether you are testing a minor product upgrade or trying to gauge the viability of a major shift in strategy, experiments are critical. They reduce risk and provide more information earlier to allow for smart decision making. Experiments have the added bonus of stimulating employee energy and creativity. The cycle from idea to results is shortened, and employees can innovate at a much more rapid pace.

Reinforce and Replicate What Works

As you begin to execute a change in strategic direction, don't wait until you achieve a major success to reward and recognize your employees. Look for any small signs of success to reinforce.

If, for example, you are looking to increase a sales team's time in front of customers from 40 percent to 80 percent of their time, send them a thank-you note when they achieve a minor improvement—say, to 45 percent. If a manufacturing team is working to improve delivery performance, recognize what they've done when they have taken the first step by figuring out how to measure delivery performance more consistently. Do this early and often, and you'll see desired changes accelerate quickly.

In Conclusion

Even the largest businesses can be agile enough to make ninety-degree turns when necessary. However, not every business is organized to deal effectively with changes in the world around them and to pounce on opportunities when they present themselves.

Adopting the **Setili Cycle of Change** can help establish agility in your organization. Make a habit of taking the following actions:

- **Communicate intent.** Painting an inspiring and vivid description of your desired future state is crucial when making a bold change in direction. The most effective companies make their vision exceptionally tangible, allowing customers, employees, investors, channel partners, and other stakeholders to see where they are headed and to help them get there.
- **Take the first steps.** All the planning or worrying in the world won't get you any closer to your goals if you don't move forward by taking action. Take the first steps, then figure out the details and make adjustments along the way.
- **Shed what doesn't fit.** Making bold moves often requires letting go of the parts of your business that are distracting, underperforming, or not supportive of your new direction. This may require you to eliminate products, brands, assets, people, customers, and more.
- **Build new capabilities.** To be agile, companies must be able to imagine a future in which they have vastly different capabilities than they do today. These capabilities may include technologies, business processes, employee skills and knowledge, and more. Organizations can acquire these in a variety of different ways, including training, technology investments, developmental career progressions, and mergers and acquisitions.
- **Experiment and reinforce.** Experimenting and learning—and then replicating or reinforcing what works best—is a critical and essential stage in implementing strategic change. Build a company culture that welcomes change and failure—one that encourages employees to conduct experiments and to try new (and more) things.

Chapter Nine

Agility as a Way of Life

Leverage the Power of Purpose, Autonomy, and Continuous Adaptation

Make no mistake about it: it's no simple task to create an agile organization in a deep-rooted, long-lasting, sustainable way. Hard work, commitment, training, process rework, top management support, employee engagement, and in some cases a complete transformation in a company's culture and in the way things are done are required. But *any* company can become an agile company using the tools presented in this book. Consider the example of a Chinese company that underwent a massive transformation to become the agile organization that it is today, one that continues to innovate and find new ways to improve.

In 1984, Zhang Ruimin, the thirty-five-year-old deputy manager for the household appliance division of the municipal government of Qingdao, China, was promoted to director of the poorly performing Qingdao Refrigerator Factory. Three other directors had tried and failed to turn around performance at the nearly bankrupt factory that year. More than eight hundred employees had not been paid in months.[1]

Thirty years later, Zhang is still serving as CEO of this appliance manufacturer—but times have definitely changed. The Qingdao Refrigerator Factory now goes by the name Haier Group, whose global revenue was $29.5 billion in 2013. Today, the Haier Group is the world's number-one major appliance brand, with a global market share of 9.7 percent.[2] According to the Haier website, the company ranked number eight on the Boston Consulting Group's 2012 Most Innovative Companies list—the only Chinese company in the top ten.

How has Haier been able to climb from being an unknown, poor-quality, state-owned domestic manufacturer to an innovative global leader? As with most flourishing organizations, it wasn't one thing but a number of things that enabled it not merely to cope with the immense market changes that have occurred over the last thirty years but to successfully exploit them.

Zhang made it clear to employees early in his tenure that *things must change.* He took bold but prudent risks—expanding early into the most demanding international markets, such as Western Europe, where Zhang believed that his company could learn as quickly as possible. He catered to niche markets where competitors were not playing. He worked to minimize the distance between customers and his employees. But perhaps most important, Zhang built Haier's culture, organizational structure, and systems to enable fast, agile responses to changes in the marketplace and to customer needs.

Shortly after he took the job of director in 1985, Zhang examined the four hundred refrigerators on the factory floor, in response to a customer complaint. Much to his dismay, he found that seventy-six—almost 20 percent—were defective. He had recently traveled to Germany to visit the company's technology suppliers, and had witnessed uniformly high levels of German product quality—so he wondered why his Chinese employees couldn't achieve the same level of quality. Zhang looks back on this time and recalls, "The real problem was that workers had no faith in the company and didn't care. Quality didn't even enter into anybody's mind."[3] Incensed, he handed out sledgehammers and joined employees in smashing every one of the seventy-six defective units in full public view. This made a deep impression on factory workers, as the price of each destroyed refrigerator was equivalent to about two years of wages.[4] Zhang's delivering this clear message to employees was an important step in the company's transformation.

In 1992, Haier began to expand internationally. Zhang followed a strategy he called "taking on the difficult one first and then the easy one."[5] In essence, he wanted Haier to first learn how to meet the most sophisticated customers' standards before exporting to less competitive regions such as Southeast Asia and Africa.[6] Focusing on demanding customers accelerated Haier's learning curve; the company was one of China's largest exporters by 2000, bringing in $2.8 billion of revenue[7] from 160 countries.[8] By the following year, Haier had established factories in twelve countries and fifteen overseas design centers.[9]

In 2000, Haier opened its factory in Camden, South Carolina. At the time, Haier was the first Chinese company to own a factory in the United States; many U.S. companies were busy moving manufacturing to China to take advantage of cheaper labor. Zhang felt strongly that locating design centers and manufacturing within the markets his company served would allow them to respond more quickly and efficiently to those markets' customers. Haier sought to understand and integrate with the local culture, but also trained its overseas workers in the Haier culture. They taught slogans developed in China, such as "quick response, immediate action."[10]

Haier was able to penetrate overseas markets rapidly and successfully due to its focus on niche markets—such as mini fridges built into computer tables for college students, and small, affordable wine coolers. Competitors intent on building economies of scale had ignored these niches, enabling Haier to gain dominant market positions. By 2000, Haier was the market share leader in wine coolers; by 2002, it offered a full line of coolers that retailed from $599 to $3,660.[11]

Haier also listened to customers and quickly adapted its products to meet their specific needs. The company discovered that farmers in parts of rural China were using their Haier clothes washers to wash their sweet potatoes. In response, Haier released a washing machine capable of washing both clothes and potatoes.[12]

As the first Chinese consumer-product brand in the United States, Haier found that customizing product in response to retailer requests was critical to breaking into the market. The brand provided easy-to-read icons on its air conditioner packaging for Target, changed wine cooler materials and handles for Home Depot, and provided locks for compact refrigerators for Office Depot to secure refrigerators placed in office cubicles and dorm rooms.[13] Customizing products not only helped Haier gain shelf space but also prevented the company from having to compete solely on price.

To meet these needs, Haier has learned to develop and customize products exceptionally quickly. During a 2001 management meeting in Qingdao, former Haier America CEO Michael Jemal scribbled a new product concept on a napkin. Within seventeen hours, the engineering team delivered a working prototype of the new product—a chest freezer with a sliding drawer—that quickly became a success in U.S. markets.[14]

The company also invests in basic research, investigating breakthrough technologies such as how to make a refrigerator that needs no compressor or a washing machine that needs no water or detergent.[15] Haier has become adept at understanding the market trends that guide its priorities for R&D. For example, the company is investing in green and low-carbon technologies, implementing "smart-home" capabilities, and mining user information to serve customers even better.[16] In January 2014, its Tianzun air conditioner became the first home appliance to get Apple's Made for iPhone/iPod/iPad (MFI) certification.[17]

Haier also utilizes extremely agile manufacturing. The company's system of on-demand manufacturing and delivery caters to changing customer demand, which allows Haier to promise customers things competitors simply cannot. For example, it can guarantee free machines if delivery is not made within twenty-four hours. Haier boasts of "zero inventory" and "zero accounts receivable." According to the Haier website, the company's cash conversion cycle—a measure of how long cash is tied up in working capital—is negative-ten days, meaning that customers pay Haier before Haier has to pay suppliers.

Perhaps the most powerful force behind Haier's agility is its novel organizational structure and unique systems for managing and motivating employees. The company's workers are split into two thousand autonomous business units called ZZJYTs (*zi zhu jing ying ti*, literally translated as "independent operation unit"). These are designed to reduce the distance between employees and customers and to empower employees to act quickly and confidently to respond to customer needs.

Tier 1 ZZJYTs are directly customer facing. Of these, there are three types:

- *Market* ZZJYTs, responsible for sales in a given region
- *Product* (or module) ZZJYTs, responsible for design, development, and marketing of products
- *Manufacturing* ZZJYTs, responsible for making precisely what is needed to meet customer demand

The system acts as a free market. For example, when Haier wishes to pursue a new market, product, or manufacturing order, the project is put up for internal auction. Each employee who wishes to lead the new ZZJYT submits a business plan containing not only his action plan and resource requirements but also the targets—such as sales and cost goals—that he is willing to commit to should he be selected to lead the ZZJYT. This ensures that employees will be ambitious to win the competition, yet realistic—because if they win, their team will be held accountable for meeting the goal.

There is an open market for talent as well. ZZJYT leaders get to select the members of their team, but employees also have the right to choose which ZZJYT they work for and the right to *dismiss their leader*. The leader evaluates team members' performance periodically, and the team members evaluate the leader. Team members also vote to choose a "catfish"—usually, the runner-up in the competition. The term comes from the lore that fishermen will put a catfish in the holding tank of the fishing boat to keep the other fish lively and fresh for the market. The catfish at Haier acts as a competitor to the team's leader, and is ready to step in should team members vote their leader out. If a team misses its targets for three consecutive months, the company automatically reconsiders the leader.

Customer-facing ZZJYTs contract with groups such as human resources, research, marketing, and finance for the support they need. Thus, the priorities of the entire seventy-thousand-employee organization are directly driven by customer needs.

It may seem like this free-market system would create chaos, but actually, the opposite is true. Haier leaders know exactly what metrics each team is responsible for. The incentive system and free market for talent motivate employees to deliver results as expected. They can make short-term adjustments either up or down based on external market changes.[18] Zhang, who dines with employees nearly every day to gain their perspectives, says, "In the past, employees waited to hear from the boss; now, they listen to the customer."[19]

This fluid but controlled system has played an important role in allowing Haier to grow quickly. "An unsteady and dynamic environment is the best way to keep everyone flexible," says Zhang. Like many of the other companies we have examined in this book, Haier has figured out how to be both big and fast at the same time.

The first eight chapters of this book explored how to identify market opportunities and develop breakthrough strategies for capturing them. We also considered how to deal with uncertainties and risks—whatever their source—and how to use the Setili Cycle of Change to manage your organization through a strategic shift.

Now we will cover what is perhaps the most important aspect of agility: executing your strategy in a flexible and adaptive way. This requires having a narrow focus to keep from becoming distracted by less important priorities. It also requires a clear vision, so that business units, functions, and employees can act in concert to achieve your goals. It means having the right people on board and actively managing your culture. It involves keeping your eye out for further market change and adapting your approach when you encounter it. And it calls for a clear and motivating purpose that will inspire and guide your employees.

Combining these elements will make your company truly agile and will lead to sustained, profitable growth—no matter what happens in *or* out of your business environment.

Create Focus by Paring Your Priorities to the Essential Few

Some companies appear to have extraordinary foresight. But in reality, they likely have no more knowledge of the future than their competitors who miss market opportunities. We can often distinguish winning from losing companies simply by their ability to communicate intent, to focus, and to stay "on task." I define focus as clearly identifying the *few things* that you are going to do, and acting deliberately and single-mindedly to achieve them.

In 2008, writer Betsy Morris flew to Hawaii to interview Apple founder and CEO Steve Jobs for a *Fortune* article. As Jobs walked down the beach with Morris, he explained the role of focus in his company's success:

> Apple is a $30 billion company, yet we've got less than 30 major products. I don't know if that's ever been done before. Certainly the great consumer electronics companies of the past had thousands of products. We tend to focus much more . . . which people think means saying yes to the thing you've got to focus on. But that's not what it means at all. It means saying no to the hundred other good ideas that there are. You have to pick carefully. I'm actually as proud of many of the things we haven't done as the things we have done.[20]

Testimony to this level of single-mindedness is that by 2012, one Apple product—the iPhone—had sales greater than those of the entire Microsoft Corporation.[21]

If you pursue too many new opportunities, your lack of focus is apt to cause them all to fail. If you go after only a few, your chances of success are much greater. I've heard my clients lament many times about their organizations' lack of focus, saying things like, "I feel like we're moving a thousand things forward an inch, instead of two or three things forward a mile." This is a common problem; although everyone loves adding a new initiative to the action plan, courage is often required to take things *off* your list. After all, you may have to go back to the boss or board of directors to explain why an initiative that seemed like a great idea when you launched it last year is no longer in the company's best interest.

Having a clear idea of the few things you are going to do and the many you are not keeps the organization from becoming scattered and overly reactive. So pare down your priorities and focus on those essential few.

Paint a Picture of the Intended Future

In 1987, a few years before Tim Berners-Lee invented the World Wide Web and introduced the very first web browser, Apple Computer prepared a remarkable video that showcased its idea of what a computer might one day look like and be able to do. Apple called this yet-to-be-invented touchscreen tablet computing device—just a concept, at the time—the Knowledge Navigator. It was a magic clipboard of sorts—easy to carry around, helping you do your job and manage your life, wherever you went. You could have a conversation with it; it would remind you of your appointments, place phone calls for you, and even dig up facts for you, such as the rate of deforestation in Brazil, or Africa's food imports. Somehow, it was connected with the world's information.

In 1987, this device looked like something in a science fiction movie—and at the time, it *was*. Apple's visionaries didn't know how to achieve this vision of the future at the time. But they imagined it and illustrated it so vividly that others could understand. (You can see the video of Apple's concept on YouTube: http://youtu.be/3WdS4TscWH8.)

Of course, we now know the rest of the story—the steps and stumbles that Apple took over the next twenty years to make that dream come true in the form of its hugely successful iPhone and iPad products. In retrospect, there can be no doubt that the *clarity* of Apple's vision was far more important than knowing exactly *how* they would get there. This was left to future Apple project managers, software developers, and hardware engineers and designers—the men and women tasked with making the company's vision real.

Painting a clear and compelling picture of the future you wish to create enables employees at all levels to make the optimal decisions daily to move toward the vision. When employees understand where you're going and why you want to go there, they make the right choices when new information or opportunities require a change in direction.

Imagine hiking through the woods and picking your way through the thick underbrush. If you can see something to head toward—a towering mountain peak off in the distance—you can make the correct decision at each turning point. If you are traveling with others and haven't communicated to them *which* mountain peak you're aiming for, your group is likely to get scattered as they encounter and respond to the obstacles they inevitably encounter—rivers, ravines, weather, and difficult terrain. But when members of the group have a common destination in mind, they're able to utilize their skills and knowledge in overcoming obstacles and taking advantage of unexpected opportunities. You'll get to the destination faster—and with your group intact.

A vividly imagined vision creates excitement in employees, as they look for ways to move the company faster in that direction. They talk about the vision with colleagues, people in other departments, suppliers, business partners, and customers. This, in turn, gives *them* ideas about what actions *they* can take to advance the cause—thereby creating a virtuous cycle.

Military leaders know that a battle plan never goes exactly as anticipated. Therefore, they always communicate a clear "commander's intent"—the purpose and desired end state of a mission that serve to guide the troops, independent of what conditions exist on the battlefield. No matter what surprises the enemy throws at them and what difficulties or lucky breaks they encounter during the heat of battle, the troops on the ground can work together to respond appropriately.

What does this have to do with building organizational agility, you might wonder?

Everything.

Much like soldiers in battle, employees who understand their leaders' intent are far more likely to get that extra shot of adrenaline needed to effectively deal with adversity. Whether the difficulties take the form of demanding and irritated customers, a new competitive offering, or an ambush on the battlefield, an unclear intent may lead individuals to subtly shut down and give up—rather than summon the extra ingenuity, instinct, and resolve to deal with the situation.

Get the Right People on Board

To be agile, you must have employees who are aligned with your vision and values—and who have or can build the capabilities you will need to succeed. It's essential to get the right people on board.

While working with a team at Walmart's company headquarters in Bentonville, Arkansas, I was very impressed by how deeply the company's values affect everything it does. Take, for example, Walmart's commitment to keeping costs low. There are no fancy accouterments and artwork or vaulted hallways of polished walnut, brass, and marble at corporate headquarters. The buildings are humble, the walls painted drywall, and the floors simple linoleum. Austere conference rooms are numbered rather than named. Reception areas and executive offices are extremely modest compared with the executive offices of most multibillion-dollar U.S. companies. Employees convey a strong and explicit recognition of what is special about the Walmart culture, especially the belief that the best ideas come up from the bottom of the organization, and a reverence for founder Sam Walton.

Walmart *has* to manage its culture very actively to achieve such strong and consistent values among its 2.2 million employees, selling $460 billion of product in twenty-seven countries.[22]

For starters, the company selects its leaders carefully. Candidates for some positions undergo a grueling and lifelike "mock day," in which actors play a variety of different roles—employees who need help solving a problem, peers seeking input, irate customers, and demanding bosses. During the day, each candidate faces one emergency and interruption after another. She must deal with these events as they occur, interacting with the actors and resolving the issues just as she would while on the job. The lunch hour ticks by with no pause in the action, and many candidates skip taking a meal break in their effort to ace the interview.

This ordeal provides prospective leaders with a taste of what they can expect in their jobs. Some don't make the cut, and others opt out, realizing that Walmart might not be the ideal environment for them. But the most important part of this process is that—combined with other evaluation criteria—it enables Walmart to identify candidates who are able to deal calmly and effectively with new and unexpected situations and to make the most of whatever comes their way.

Your organization may have a different but equally effective process for selecting employees. The important thing is that you choose and retain individuals who are aligned with your values and who have the resilience, energy, and desire to create and sustain agility. As Jim Collins says in *Good to Great*: "The executives who ignited transformation [within their companies] did not first figure out where to drive the bus and then get people to take it there. No, they first got the right people on the bus (and the wrong people off the bus) and then figured out where to drive it."[23]

Set an Example for Employee Behavior

Delta was named the most admired airline in the world by *Fortune* magazine in 2013.[24] However, it's certainly had its ups and downs over the years. In the early 2000s, Delta was on a downswing. Employees were angry and frustrated with management, which showed in the level of service and less than stellar experiences customers received.

Yet Delta's employees believed in "service from the heart"—the ethos that had been at the company's core for decades. It is a feeling that anyone who walks down the halls of Delta's corporate headquarters in Atlanta can experience. The company's employees are warm and friendly, and it is a very pleasant place to be.

Leaders sometimes fail to realize the impact that they can have on their organization and on its culture. They can guide employee attitudes and behaviors, and mold corporate cultures. When Delta merged with Northwest Airlines in 2008, Richard Anderson became CEO—and did an outstanding job of creating a unified culture that retained the best aspects of each company's culture. He preserved Delta's spirit of service while injecting Northwest's discipline and rigor. To aid this cultural shift, Anderson created a booklet called "Rules of the Road." Building on a document written by Delta's first CEO, C. E. Woolman, Anderson included rules such as "Attack the biggest issues first and never give up"; "Know the competition, respect the competition and be humble"; and "Connect with our customers. Superior customer service and relationships can be a strategic advantage that allows us to beat our competitors."

Some rules of the road are practical—more like career advice than what you would normally expect from a corporate rule book: "Avoid long, flashy presentations—if we cannot be concise and reach a substantial conclusion in ten pages of well-written and organized thinking, then rethink the problem and solution." Some are philosophical: "Each of us has the opportunity every day to be a leader in how we represent Delta, how we handle difficult and unpredictable situations."

These rules guide how employees at Delta get work done and make decisions. Employees refer to the rules during meetings; these guidelines help the senior team establish a sense of culture and conduct. Each employee who works at headquarters has a copy with his or her name on it, and people who stray from the rules in meetings are called out for it. Delta expects full disclosure and timely communication from its employees, especially when things aren't going as planned. Transparency and cross-functional communication allow employees to better support each other to fix problems.

Of course, leaders of other top-performing U.S. companies also know the power of modeling behaviors to manage culture. Home Depot executives wear the company's trademark orange aprons—even in their offices. Executives at insurance company Cigna Group have been known to personally push coffee carts around the office, serving refreshments to employees during busy times of the year; and Southwest Airlines chairman emeritus Herb Kelleher regularly pitched in to help flight attendants serve beverages to customers when he flew on his airline. Think about your leadership team for a moment. What behaviors do *you* model to your people?

Motivate Through Autonomy and Empowerment

We live in a world where creativity is paramount. Operational excellence—keeping costs low and making a consistent, quality product—is still very important, but it's no longer enough. Only companies that continuously keep an eye out for new opportunities and adjust course as the market changes will survive.

"Pay for performance" incentives of the past relied on the ability to predict, often months ahead of time, what "numbers" each business unit, team, or employee should be able to hit, if they expended maximum effort. However, we often can't predict what goals are best. Setting a goal too high can be disappointing because there is no chance of "making bonus." If we set the goal too low, it's too easy to achieve—and employees can coast through the last part of the year. How can we best motivate employees in a world where things are changing so fast, and creativity is so critical?

Daniel Pink explains in his book *Drive* that unless an employee's work requires little to no creativity, financial incentives often lead to *worse* performance. He identifies three elements of true motivation:

- *Autonomy*: the urge to direct our own lives and to have control over our work
- *Mastery*: the desire to get increasingly better at something that matters
- *Purpose*: the desire to do what we do while serving something larger than ourselves

Luckily, all three of these employee "wants" are perfectly aligned with the needs of an agile company. We *need* our people to work autonomously (at least to a certain extent), so that they can adapt without us telling them to. We need employees to get better and better at their work to continually enhance our organizational capabilities and efficiency. And we of course want employees to do what they do in service of something larger than themselves; that is how we can become a dynamic, collaborative, and agile organization.

Teresa Amabile and Steven Kramer's book, *The Progress Principle, Using Small Wins to Ignite Joy, Engagement, and Creativity at Work*, explains that making progress in meaningful work is the most important factor driving employee happiness and motivation—two outcomes that in turn lead to creative productivity. Amabile and Kramer explain that the best way for employees to know that they have made progress in their work is to get feedback *from the work itself*. The authors explain, "The key, then, is to design each job so that, in the act of carrying out the work, people gain knowledge about the results of their effort."[25]

This feedback loop, by which employees know that they are making progress, and are motivated by that progress, is an essential component of agility.

Let's go back to Delta Air Lines for a moment—a company that has worked hard in recent years to create "situational flexibility." Delta trains employees on the company's overall intent—say, to rebook passengers in the minimum time possible when a flight is cancelled—and has given them increased power and authority to make on-the-spot decisions. When an employee is face-to-face with an anxious passenger who is trying to make it home or to a business meeting, or who hopes to arrive at his or her vacation destination before it's time to turn around and come back, the employee is able to solve passenger problems without taking the time to check with management—in an industry where every minute counts.

Delta employees are motivated by a common purpose—to give great service and a remarkable customer experience. This purpose is well aligned with the natural inclination of the people whom Delta selects through their daylong interview process: individuals who are inherently oriented to pleasing others. Employees who feel good about what they are accomplishing together smile more often and perform better. And when employees smile more, passengers treat them better, creating a virtuous cycle—a feedback loop—that leads to even greater motivation and better performance.

Agile companies should instill the intrinsic motivation of enjoying a degree of autonomy (either as an individual, as a group, or as a business unit), growing in capability, and making progress toward achieving a greater purpose. If you create those conditions, you will keep your most ingenious and capable employees *and* achieve the agility needed to create and sustain a competitive advantage.

Plan for the Unexpected

Incentive-based pay systems are appropriate in many situations, and they will continue to be a part of our business life for many years to come. To ensure that your incentives help rather than hinder your agility, take steps to build flexibility into them.

Here is an example of a common dilemma in fast-changing markets: your company discovers a fabulous new technology midway through the year. Because of the growth opportunity this represents, you would like to buy the rights to it before your competitor does. If you use an annual budget cycle, with performance-based incentives, managers have three choices:

- Put money in the budget for next year, and hope that the opportunity is still available.
- Invest now. (But the unplanned expense will reduce the managers' bonus compensation.)

- Cut back on spending in another area in order to free up funds for investment this year. (However, you are likely to damage performance in that other area by robbing it of funds.)

Each of these choices has major disadvantages—but you can mitigate them all by setting aside funds in the budget each year to be used for *unexpected opportunities*. You may also wish to provide special bonuses for managers who adapt effectively to changing conditions. And you can set appropriate metrics (perhaps based on achieving certain learning objectives or milestones) for managers who are responsible for high-risk growth initiatives.

The point is that you can and should *plan for the unexpected*. Doing so will enable you to react to fast-moving markets without stealing funds from your incentive pools or other important budget items. Although you may not be able to anticipate exactly what form these events and opportunities will take when they arise—nor their potential financial impact—you will be able to take action immediately if you reserve a part of your budget to respond to them.

Improve and Adapt Continuously

The agile organization innovates continuously, constantly improving product offerings, processes, and organizational capability. The process of continuous improvement enables us to adjust course as our customers' needs and the business environment change—reducing our risk of becoming obsolete or allowing competitors to preempt us.

Google, for example, makes continuous upgrades to its online products such as Gmail, Google Maps, and the Google search algorithm. Because most changes are small, they're not disruptive to users. Contrast that approach with Microsoft's: when they release a new Windows operating system once every two or three years, users often struggle to cope with many major changes at once, and many choose to defer an upgrade for months or even years.

Companies can even continuously upgrade durable goods such as cars. Tesla's Model S sedan downloads software updates on a regular basis. These changes are not limited to superficial user interface elements like the dashboard or navigation system; they can even alter the car's suspension, acceleration, or handling characteristics. Tesla has even abandoned the standard automotive industry concept of model years, opting to instead *continually* improve its products' physical design and assembly process.[26]

In the future, we can expect faster rates of change in the way we hire and manage our employees, collaborate with colleagues, communicate with suppliers and customers, and get our products to market, and in other elements of our business system. We must continuously adapt by observing our environment, assessing our options, deciding on a path forward, and taking action.

The Importance of a Motivating Purpose

One of the most innovative and highly competitive product categories that I've witnessed—and worked in—is the disposable diaper category. Employees in this industry have a clear purpose: improving life for babies and their caregivers.

It's easy to see why diaper consumers value innovation so highly. Keeping baby happy and furniture and clothing clean is immensely valuable, compared to the alternative. And with 130 million new babies arriving annually, market share can be won and lost quickly. Kimberly-Clark and Procter & Gamble's race to innovate and to capture a greater percentage of this new crop of infants each year has fueled each company's competitive spirit for decades.

When P&G's head of the Exploratory Development Group, Vic Mills, spent a weekend in 1956 changing his grandson's cloth diapers, he realized there had to be a better way. Mills convinced P&G to invest in developing a disposable diaper affordable enough, at six cents per diaper, to use every day.[27]

The product—introduced in 1961 and called Pampers—was revolutionary. By the mid-1970s, P&G enjoyed a 75 percent share of the U.S. disposable diaper market and had expanded the Pampers brand to seventy-five countries worldwide.

In 1976, P&G introduced a new brand called Luvs. It was priced 30 percent higher than Pampers, but had better fit, absorbency, and comfort. Pampers immediately began to lose share to its sister brand. Within two years, a threat to P&G's enviable position emerged when Kimberly-Clark came out with Huggies in 1978. This new brand had a better fit, an improved tape fastening system, and enhanced absorbency. With P&G splitting its energy and brand-building dollars between two competing brands, and Huggies priced between Pampers and Luvs, Huggies' market share climbed rapidly.[28] By the late 1980s, Huggies surpassed Pampers to become the leading disposable diaper brand.[29]

With its flagship Pampers brand losing share every year, P&G invested $750 million to develop and introduce a new offering, Pampers Ultra, with features similar to Huggies and Luvs.[30] By that time, however, Huggies was firmly entrenched, and P&G found itself in the unfortunate position of having two virtually identical products in the market. The company struggled for another decade to differentiate the two products with advertising, but was unsuccessful. Finally, in 1994, P&G threw in the towel by repositioning Luvs as a budget brand.

While P&G was grappling with branding decisions and manufacturing investments, Kimberly-Clark stayed busy innovating new superabsorbent technologies. In 1992, the company introduced a dramatically thinner Huggies Ultra Trim product. It took P&G more than a year to come out with its own Pampers Ultra Dry Thin product—enough time for Huggies to again make a sharp gain in market share.

I have a long-standing personal connection with Kimberly-Clark's disposable diaper business. When my father worked there as an engineer, he was a member of the team given the task of developing a better disposable diaper—and I was the test baby. Years later, I was an engineer for Kimberly-Clark too; and like my father, I worked on improving the company's disposable diapers.

What enabled Kimberly-Clark to be so agile, to capture share from its highly capable competitor at numerous points in time? Both companies were remarkably innovative. Both were smart. Both relied on diapers for an enormous share of their total corporate profits, so this was the category to win—the most important battlefield either company competed on.

There was really no magic formula or special trick; the truth is, Kimberly-Clark just *kept at it*. Its employees worked hard to understand how they could make customers' lives easier. They invited parents and babies to play at the corporate campus's play center. When it was time to change the babies' diapers, Kimberly-Clark scientists examined the used ones to measure and observe each aspect of the product's performance—how much it absorbed, whether it leaked, and whether there were gaps around the legs or waist when the diaper was fitted to different sizes and shapes of babies. Was the liner dry against the baby's skin, to protect from rashes? Did it hold its shape and not bunch up after hours of playing? They found out what mattered most to moms and dads. They talked to suppliers and to Kimberly-Clark's own machine operators and quality testers. They were systematic and relentless in their innovation. They observed, they measured, they took notes, they planned, and they acted.

My experience at Kimberly-Clark taught me the value of having a clear sense of purpose. I worked every day with people from marketing, operations, finance, product development, production planning, maintenance, and logistics. We all had different jobs, but we had a shared purpose: to keep babies dry and safe.

This purpose—the "why" behind everything we did—made it fun to collaborate with my colleagues from other departments. Each innovation—adding comfortable stretch sides, improving the refastenable closures so that parents could check the diaper without removing it, improving the wicking and fluid-barrier properties of the liner, adding wetness indicators—was exciting. Even the ho-hum daily routine of testing incoming raw materials and finished product, taking inventory, and running the production line was enjoyable and satisfying for us.

The customer was always top of mind—more than our shareholders and our own compensation. We wanted to reduce prices so that more people could benefit from the product we made. We knew that if we could drive cost down, there would be plenty of money available for investment in R&D and for spreading the word about our great products via marketing investments. As testament to this unwavering focus on increasing product performance while bringing down costs, Kimberly-Clark diaper operating income improved from 16 percent of sales in 1988 to 28 percent in 2002. We simultaneously grew top-line revenue while growing our bottom-line profit. Not many companies are able to accomplish such a feat.[31]

Your purpose explains *why* you do what you do. This "why" provides energy, resiliency, and determination in the face of market upsets. People who care about the "why" behind their work are more curious, creative, and observant. They see new opportunities as they emerge, and they collaborate to capture them. Ensure that your employees understand and believe in the purpose of their work, and they will execute your strategy with passion and resiliency.

In Conclusion

Agility isn't something you can leave to chance. To be consistently and effectively agile, you must take a number of specific actions, including the following:

- **Create focus.** Paring your priorities down to a few things you are going to do (and many you are not) enhances your agility by keeping the organization from becoming scattered and overly reactive. Focus on the few things you've deemed most critical.

- **Communicate a clear vision of your intended future.** For organizations to be agile, employees need to know where they are going together. It's up to a company's leaders to create a clear vision which describes that destination in a vibrant and emotionally appealing way. Employees adapt to market change daily, making many small—or large—decisions each day. When they understand the big-picture objectives, they make the right decisions when new opportunities emerge.

- **Hire the right people and deploy them in the most effective way.** Agility depends on employees being fully aligned with your company's vision and values. Get the right people on board and then be sure they're doing the things that bring greatest value to your business—and your customers.

- **Set an example.** Your company's culture should reflect its values, and your role as a leader is to raise the bar high through your own actions and behavior. Be transparent, communicate widely and often, and put serving your employees and customers at the top of your daily to-do list.

- **Enhance autonomy.** To increase motivation, creativity, and agility, give employees control over how they complete their work, and provide feedback loops so that employees know when they are making progress.

- **Plan for the unexpected.** Build flexibility into your budgeting and incentive systems by setting aside funds that can be used to pursue unexpected opportunities. Set appropriate metrics, based on learning objectives, for managers who are responsible for high-risk growth initiatives.

- **Implement continuous innovation.** Rather than limiting your product or service innovations for some arbitrary period of time and then introducing your "new-and-improved" this or that, continuously innovate, improve, and enhance in real time as these ideas develop. Your business will be light on its feet and constantly moving as a result, and you'll be better able to respond to customer needs and technological change.

- **Create a motivating purpose.** Everyone wants to feel that her job is important and that she is working for an organization that is having a real and positive impact on the world. Ensure that your employees understand and believe in the purpose of their work, so that they can execute your strategy with passion and resiliency.

Conclusion

As we reach the last few pages of this book, I hope to have convinced you of two things.

First, I hope that you now fully understand the important role that agility plays in the survival and continued growth of organizations today. As the many examples in this book illustrate, companies of all shapes and sizes are focusing no small amount of time and money on improving their agility. Their leaders know that if they don't, then their more agile competitors will leave them behind.

Second, I hope you now have the information and knowledge you will need to embark on your own path toward organizational agility. I have presented a variety of frameworks, examples, techniques, and more to provide you with all the tools you will need to succeed. It's now up to you to apply them.

It's no secret that change is rampant today. I wrote this book because I noticed that a number of companies I worked with were having difficulty dealing with market change, and that this difficulty was threatening their bottom line. Every organization today—no matter its size, industry, or offering—can benefit from becoming more agile. You now have a tool kit you can use to better spot and capture new opportunities while more effectively leveraging your people and your financial resources.

This book is just the beginning. As a complementary supplement to this text, I offer a wealth of information—including frameworks, tools, techniques, and case studies—online for your use at www.theagilityadvantage.net. In addition, my consulting firm, Setili & Associates (http://setiliandassociates.com), is available to work with you if you have any questions about how to implement the techniques presented in this book. We have years of experience with some of the world's leading companies, including Delta Air Lines, Coca-Cola, United Parcel Service, Walmart, The Home Depot, Wachovia, Equifax, and others.

Writing this book has been a remarkable and rewarding experience for me. I will have reached my goal if you put the techniques I describe in this book to work in your organization and as a result find the success you are looking for. Please send me your success stories as your organization becomes more agile—I can't wait to read them.

Notes

Chapter 1

1. Jason Hiner, "GE's $200 Million Bet to Resurrect IT," TechRepublic, November 30, 2012, http://www.techrepublic.com/blog/tech-sanity-check/ges-200-million-bet-to-resurrect-it/.

2. Charles Fishmannov, "The Insourcing Boom," *Atlantic*, December 2012, http://www.theatlantic.com/magazine/archive/2012/12/the-insourcing-boom/309166/.

3. Will Connors, "Multiple Missteps Led to RIM's Fall," *Wall Street Journal*, June 28, 2012, http://online.wsj.com/news/articles/SB10001424052702304458604577488610583090408.

4. Anders Bylund, "Fresh Air or Sell Signal? Chairman Admits Intel Fumbled the Mobile Market," Motley Fool, November 22, 2013, http://www.fool.com/investing/general/2013/11/22/fresh-air-or-sell-signal-chairman-admits-that-inte.aspx.

5. Eric Pfanner, "Music Industry Sales Rise, and Digital Revenue Gets the Credit," *New York Times*, February 26, 2013, http://www.nytimes.com/2013/02/27/technology/music-industry-records-first-revenue-increase-since-1999.html?_r=0.

6. "Digital Media: Counting the Change," *Economist*, August 17, 2013, http://www.economist.com/news/business/21583687-media-companies-took-battering-internet-cash-digital-sources-last.

7. Steve Knopper, "The New Economics of the Music Industry: How Artists Really Make Money in the Cloud—or Don't," *Rolling Stone*, October 25, 2011, http://www.rollingstone.com/music/news/the-new-economics-of-the-music-industry-20111025.

8. Rick Edmonds, Emily Guskin, Amy Mitchell, and Mark Jurkowitz, "Newspapers: Stabilizing, but Still Threatened," The State of

the News Media, Pew Research Center's Project for Excellence in Journalism (July 18, 2013), http://stateofthemedia.org/2013/newspapers-stabilizing-but-still-threatened/newspapers-by-the-numbers/.

9. John Reeves, "Jeff Bezos' Plan to Save the Washington Post," Motley Fool, October 5, 2013, http://www.fool.com/investing/general/2013/10/05/how-jeff-bezos-will-fix-the-washington-post.aspx.

10. Jennifer Saba, "Amazon's Bezos Pays Hefty Price for Washington Post," Reuters, August 7, 2013, http://www.reuters.com/article/2013/08/07/us-washingtonpost-bezos-idUSBRE9740Y420130807.

11. This price appeared in a 1950 Sears Craftsman ad in *Popular Mechanics*, as seen on the Vintage Machinery website, accessed May 13, 2014, http://vintagemachinery.org/mfgindex/imagedetail.aspx?id=1623. The Bureau of Labor Statistics CPI inflation calculator (http://www.bls.gov/data/inflation_calculator.htm) was used to calculate the equivalent 2013 price. My thanks to Miki Vuckovic, product innovation strategist at Robert Bosch Tool Corporation, for bringing this excellent example to light.

12. Kurt Eichenwald, "The Great Smartphone War," *Vanity Fair*, June 2014, http://www.vanityfair.com/business/2014/06/apple-samsung-smartphone-patent-war.

13. "Hard Knocks," *Economist*, August 17, 2013, http://www.economist.com/news/business/21583663-department-stores-have-been-losing-customers-other-retailers-decades-some-are.

Chapter 2

1. Lashinsky, A., "Amazon's Jeff Bezos: The Ultimate Disrupter," *Fortune*, December 3, 2012, 100.

2. Daniel Eran Dilger, "IDC Data Shows 66% of Android's 81% Smartphone Share Are Junk Phones Selling for $215," *AppleInsider*, November 12, 2013, http://appleinsider.com/articles/13/11/12/idc-data-shows-66-of-androids-81-smartphone-share-are-junk-phones-selling-for-215.

3. Betsy Morris, "Steve Jobs Speaks Out," *Fortune*, March 2008, http://money.cnn.com/galleries/2008/fortune/0803/gallery.jobsqna.fortune/index.html.

4. Amazon Services, Seller Forums, "Thread: Is the new Amazon layout giving anyone else difficulty when listing?" posted July 2, 2013, https://sellercentral.amazon.com/forums/thread.jspa?threadID=174287&tstart=0.

5. Siko Bouterse, "Submissions/IdeaLab Brainstorm," Wikimania 2013, Submission No. 3038, Subject Number W1, August 9, 2013, http://wikimania2013.wikimedia.org/wiki/Submissions/IdeaLab_Brainstorm.

Chapter 3

1. Youngme Moon and John Quelch, "Starbucks: Delivering Customer Service," Harvard Business School case, July 31, 2003, Prod. #: 504016-PDF-ENG, available at http://hbr.org/product /starbucks-delivering-customer-service/an/504016-PDF-ENG.

2. Starbucks, "Starbucks Company Profile," January 2014, http:// news.starbucks.com/uploads/documents/AboutUs-Company Profile-Q4-2013.pdf.

3. Starbucks Corporation, *Fiscal 2013 Annual Report*, iv, accessible at http://investor.starbucks.com/phoenix.zhtml?c=99518&p=irol -reportsannual.

4. Marcy Nicholson (Reuters), "Americans Are Getting Even More Pretentious About How They Drink Coffee," *Huffington Post*, March 22, 2014, http://www.huffingtonpost.com/2014/03/22 /coffee-drinking-americans_n_5013544.html.

5. Walter Loeb, "Starbucks: Global Coffee Giant Has New Growth Plans," *Forbes*, January 31, 2013, http://www.forbes.com /sites/walterloeb/2013/01/31/starbucks-global-coffee-giant-has -new-growth-plans/.

6. Melissa Allison, "Starbucks Has a New Growth Strategy—More Revenue with Lower Costs," *Seattle Times*, May 15, 2010, http:// seattletimes.com/html/businesstechnology/2011861321_starbucks strategy16.html.

7. "Starbucks Gains Leadership in Nearly $1 Billion Light Roast Coffee Segment," January 6, 2013, Starbucks Newsroom, http:// news.starbucks.com/news/starbucks-gains-leadership-in-nearly -1-billion-light-roast-coffee-segment.

8. Jon Gertner, "Most Innovative Companies 2012: 24_Starbucks," *Fast Company*, February 7, 2012, http://www.fastcompany.com /3017375/most-innovative-companies-2012/24starbucks.

9. "Tea: Consumption: Countries Compared," NationMaster.com, Global Market Information Database, Euromonitor, 2002, http:// www.nationmaster.com/country-info/stats/Lifestyle/Food-and -drink/Tea/Consumption; and "Tea and Malaysia," Teaauction .com, http://www.teauction.com/industry/malaytea.asp.

10. "Per Capita GDP at Current Prices—US Dollars," Malaysia, 1995, National Accounts Estimates of Main Aggregates, United Nations Statistics Division, accessed June 10, 2014, http://data.un.org /Data.aspx?d=SNAAMA&f=grID%3A101%3BcurrID%3AUSD %3BpcFlag%3A1.

11. Jacqueline Toyad and Elaine Lau, "Datuk Farah Khan," *Edge Malaysi*, September 7, 2009, http://www.theedgemalaysia.com /lifestyle/150193-cover-story-datuk-farah-khan.pdf.

12. Garmin Ltd., "Financial Review," *2013 Annual Report*, http://sites
     .garmin.com/annualreport/.
13. Garmin Ltd., "World Wide PND Market Trends," *2012 Annual
     Report*, http://www8.garmin.com/aboutGarmin/invRelations
     /reports/2012_Annual_Report.pdf.
14. "The Pet Services Industry Today," ZoomRoom, retrieved May 31,
     2014, http://www.zoomroomonline.com/pet-services.html. Note 1
     for this article references "Industry Statistics & Trends," *2011–2012
     National Pet Owners Survey*, American Pet Products Association,
     2011.
15. Emily Glazer, "PetSmart Thrives by Treating Owners Like
     Parents," *Wall Street Journal*, September 11, 2012, http://online
     .wsj.com/news/articles/SB1000087239639044369660457764561
     1691766788.
16. Eileen Brown, "IBM Announces Customer Tools to Keep the
     CMO and CIO Happy," ZDNet, July 23, 2012, http://www.zdnet
     .com/ibm-announces-customer-tools-to-keep-the-cmo-and-cio
     -happy-7000001406/.
17. Andrew King and Karim R. Lakhani, "Using Open Innovation
     to Identify the Best Ideas," *MIT Sloan Management Review*,
     September 11, 2013, http://sloanreview.mit.edu/article/using
     -open-innovation-to-identify-the-best-ideas/.

Chapter 4

1. All quotations and information related to Airbnb are from Joe
    Gebbia, speaking at a meeting of the Brookhaven Chamber of
    Commerce, Brookhaven, Georgia, September 6, 2013.
2. Matt Rushing, vice president, Global Advanced Technology
    Solutions Product Line, speaking at the Product Development
    and Management Association Georgia Summit, Atlanta, Georgia,
    September 27, 2012.
3. Gerardo Garcia, group director, global design, the Coca-Cola
    Company, speaking at the Product Development and Manage-
    ment Association Georgia Summit, Atlanta, Georgia, September
    27, 2012.
4. Interview with Ross McCullough, UPS president of corporate
    strategy, on November 15, 2013.
5. Hala Moddelmog, speaking at Harvard Business School Club of
    Atlanta Women's Special Interest Group meeting, Atlanta, Geor-
    gia, October 18, 2012.
6. Abigail Phillips, "Interview with Arby's Hala Moddelmog," *Food
    Digital*, March 26, 2013, http://www.fooddigital.com/franchising
    /interview-with-arbys-hala-moddelmog.

7.   Ibid.
8.   Melissa French, "Arby's Bites Back," *Profile*, October/November/
     December 2013, http://profilemagazine.com/2013/arbys-bites
     -back/.
9.   Erin Dostal, "Arby's Targets 'Modern Day Traditionalists,'"
     Nation's Restaurant News, March 7, 2013, http://nrn.com/latest
     -headlines/arby-s-targets-modern-day-traditionalists.
10. Moddelmog, Harvard Business School Club of Atlanta speech.
11. "MAC President & CEO," profile of Hala Moddelmog, Metro
     Atlanta Chamber, accessed May 31, 2014, http://www.metro
     atlantachamber.com/about/mac/president.

Chapter 5

1.   Mark Kennan, "The History of FedEx," eHow, accessed Novem-
     ber 3, 2013, http://www.ehow.com/about_5438942_history-fedex
     .html#ixzz2jXGNXJV1.
2.   UPS, *UPS Overview: Investor Relations*, May 2014, accessible at
     http://www.investors.ups.com/phoenix.zhtml?c=62900&p=irol
     -investorpres.
3.   UPS is both a competitor and customer of the USPS, using the
     USPS for "last-mile delivery" in many markets under the UPS
     SurePost brand.
4.   Jordan Crook, "What Happened to Kodak's Moment?" Tech
     Crunch, January 21, 2012, http://techcrunch.com/2012/01/21
     /what-happened-to-kodaks-moment/.
5.   "UPS: 'All In' for Natural Gas," *Commercial Carrier Journal*, June
     26, 2013, http://www.ccjdigital.com/ups-all-in-for-natural-gas/.
6.   David Abney, "The UPS Journey: Lessons from 300 Million Green
     Miles," UPS Pressroom, accessed May 31, 2014, http://www.press
     room.ups.com/About+UPS/UPS+Leadership/Speeches/David
     +Abney/ci.The+UPS+Journey%3A+Lessons+from+300
     +Million+Green+Miles.print.
7.   Jeff Berman, "Are Regional Entrants Storming the Gates?" *Logis-
     tics Management*, July 2012, http://logisticsmgmt.com/images/site
     /LM1201_TransBP_ParcelExpRT.pdf.

Chapter 6

1.   Cliff Kuang, "Six Bite-Sized Innovation Lessons from eBay's New
     Design Think Tank," *Co.DESIGN* (blog), *Fast Company*, January
     25, 2012, http://www.fastcodesign.com/1664404/six-bite-sized
     -innovation-lessons-from-ebays-new-design-think-tank.

2. "Mortality: Road Traffic Deaths Data by Country," World Health Organization, Global Health Observatory Data Repository, accessed May 14, 2014, http://apps.who.int/gho/data/node.main .A997.

3. Michael Norton, Daniel Mochon, and Dan Ariely, "The IKEA Effect: When Labor Leads to Love," *Journal of Consumer Psychology* 22, no. 3 (July 2012): 453–460.

4. Susan Cain, "Rise of the New Groupthink," *New York Times*, January 15, 2012, http://www.nytimes.com/2012/01/15/opinion /sunday/the-rise-of-the-new-groupthink.html?pagewanted=all& _r=0.

5. Derrick Harris, "The Secret to Amazon's Cloud Success Might Be Jeff Bezos' Corporate Culture," Gigaom, November 18, 2013, http://gigaom.com/2013/11/18/the-secret-to-amazons-cloud -success-might-be-jeff-bezos-corporate-culture/.

6. "Pearlfinder Frequently Asked Questions," Beiersdorf AG, accessed June 1, 2014, http://pearlfinder.beiersdorf.com/faqs.

7. Andrew King and Karim Lakhani, "Using Open Innovation to Identify the Best Ideas," *MIT Sloan Management Review*, September 11, 2013, http://sloanreview.mit.edu/article/using -open-innovation-to-identify-the-best-ideas/.

8. Dane Howard, director, global brand experience at eBay, "Power of PreVIZ," March 11, 2012, Slideshare.com, http://www.slideshare .net/fubdog/the-power-of-previz.

9. Dane Howard, Optimizing Innovation conference, New York, October 23, 2013.

Chapter 7

1. "Elon Musk: Tesla Motors CEO, Stanford GSB 2013 Entrepreneurial Company of the Year," video of 36th annual ENCORE Award event, Stanford Graduate School of Business, October 2, 2013, https://www.youtube.com/watch?v=MBItc _QAUUM.

2. Jessica Caldwell, "Drive by Numbers—Tesla Model S Is the Vehicle of Choice in Many of America's Wealthiest Zip Codes," Edmunds.com, October 31, 2013, http://www.edmunds.com /industry-center/analysis/drive-by-numbers-tesla-model-s-is-the -vehicle-of-choice-in-many-of-americas-wealthiest-zip-codes .html.

3. David S. Kidder, *The Startup Playbook* (San Francisco: Chronicle Books, 2012), 217.

4. David Undercoffler, "Tesla Motors Plans to Debut Cheaper Car in Early 2015," *Los Angeles Times*, December 15, 2013, http://www

.latimes.com/business/autos/la-fi-hy-autos-tesla-model-e-debut
-2015-20131213,0,37648.story#axzz2ne2JusZJ.

5. Tamara Rutter, "Tesla's Supercharger Network: Next Stop, World
    Domination," Motley Fool, November 19, 2013, http://www.fool
    .com/investing/general/2013/11/19/teslas-supercharger-network
    -next-stop-world-domina.aspx.

6. Clara Moskowitz, "SpaceX Unveils Plan for World's Most Powerful
    Private Rocket," SPACE.com, April 5, 2011, http://www
    .space.com/11298-spacex-rocket-private-spaceflight-falcon9
    .html.

7. Associated Press, "Tesla Model S Crash Test Ads Prompt NHTSA
    to Change Rules," November 21, 2013, http://article.wn.com/view
    /2013/11/21/Tesla_Model_S_crash_test_ads_prompt_NHTSA
    _to_change_rules/.

8. Chris Anderson, "The Shared Genius of Elon Musk and Steve
    Jobs," *Fortune*, December 9, 2013, http://fortune.com/2013/11/21
    /the-shared-genius-of-elon-musk-and-steve-jobs/.

Chapter 8

1. Jonathan Cheng and Min-Jeong Lee, "Samsung Is Getting
    Squeezed," *Wall Street Journal*, January 8, 2014, http://online.wsj
    .com/news/articles/SB20001424052702304617404579305723355
    535440.

2. Koon Boon Kee, "New Year's Greetings by Asian Patriarchs:
    Implications for Value Investors," Beyond Proxy, January 6, 2014,
    http://www.beyondproxy.com/new-years-greetings/.

3. Jim Collins, *Good to Great* (New York: HarperBusiness, 2001), 169.

4. Glenn Lurie, speaking at Setili & Associates Strategic Agility
    Think Tank event, March 16, 2012.

5. Ibid.

6. Glenn Lurie, interviewed by Walt Mossberg, on "D: Dive into
    Mobile: The Full Interview Video of AT&T's Glenn Lurie,"
    AllThingsD video, December 28, 2010, posted by Kara Swisher.
    http://allthingsd.com/20101228/d-dive-into-mobile-the-full
    -interview-video-of-atts-glenn-lurie/.

7. Michael Endler, "Cisco CEO: We're All In on Internet of
    Everything," InformationWeek, February 25, 2013, http://www
    .informationweek.com/software/information-management/cisco
    -ceo-were-all-in-on-internet-of-everything/d/d-id/1108801?.

8. Don Clark, "Internet of Things in Reach," *Wall Street Journal*,
    January 6, 2014, http://online.wsj.com/news/articles/SB10001424
    052702303640604579296580892973264.

9. Sarah Mitroff, "What AT&T Learned from Apple and Amazon: 10 Questions with Glenn Lurie," *Wired*, August 9, 2012, http://www.wired.com/business/2012/08/glenn-lurie/.

10. Lurie, Strategic Agility Think Tank event.

11. Clayton M. Christensen, Scott D. Anthony, and Erik A. Roth, *Seeing What's Next: Using the Theories of Innovation to Predict Industry Change* (Boston: Harvard Business School Press, 2004), xxi.

12. Home Depot, "News Release: Home Depot Presents 2007 Key Priorities and Financial Outlook," February 28, 2007, http://phx.corporate-ir.net/phoenix.zhtml?c=63646&p=irol-newsArticle&ID=1267173&highlight=.

13. David Strasser, Sarang Vora, and Darren Bassman, "The Home Depot; Making It Look Simple," Janney Capital Markets, August 14, 2012. (Document available from Janney upon request.)

14. "Ford Renews Passenger Cars, CUVs and Minivans Using Volvo and Mazda Platforms," MarkLines Automotive Industry Portal, February 7, 2006, http://www.marklines.com/en/report/rep447_200602.

15. Mary Schlangenstein and Mary Jane Credeur, "Southwest to Unload AirTran's Boeing 717s with Delta Leases," *Bloomberg*, May 22, 2012, http://www.bloomberg.com/news/2012-05-22/southwest-agrees-to-sublease-88-boeing-717-jets-to-delta-air.html.

16. Lisa DiCarlo, "How Lou Gerstner Got IBM to Dance," *Forbes*, November 11, 2002, retrieved June 2, 2014, from http://www.forbes.com/2002/11/11/cx_ld_1112gerstner.html.

17. Jeffrey Sprecher, CEO, Intercontinental Exchange, speaking at the Leadership Breakfast Series, Harvard Business School Club of Georgia, December 19, 2012.

18. Gene Kim, "Why Every Company Needs a DevOps Team Now," *FeldThoughts* (blog), July 8, 2013, http://www.feld.com/wp/archives/2013/07/why-every-company-needs-a-devops-team-now.html.

Chapter 9

1. Zhang Ruimin, "Raising Haier," *Harvard Business Review*, February 2007, http://hbr.org/2007/02/raising-haier/ar/1.

2. Haier, "News & Press: Haier Ranks as No. 1 Global Major Appliances Brand for 5th Consecutive Year," July 1, 2014, http://www.haier.com/uk/newspress/pressreleases/201401/t20140107_204053.shtml.

3. "Zhang Ruimin, CEO, Haier Group, China," *BloombergBusinessWeek*, June 14, 1999, http://www.businessweek.com/1999/99_24/b3633071.htm

4. Wang Yantian and Song Xuechun, "Haier Rises Through Reform and Opening Up," *People's Daily*, August 8, 2001, http://english .peopledaily.com.cn/200202/19/print20020219_90595.html.

5. Ibid.

6. "Haier and Higher: The Radical Boss of Haier Wants to Transform the World's Biggest Appliance-Maker into a Nimble Internet-Age Firm," *Economist*, October 12, 2013, http://www.economist.com /news/business/21587792-radical-boss-haier-wants-transform -worlds-biggest-appliance-maker-nimble.

7. Yuping Du, "Haier's Survival Strategy to Compete with World Giants," *Journal of Chinese Economic and Business Studies*, February 2003, http://www.ryerson.ca/~iri/papers/ypdu.pdf.

8. Mark Landler, "In China, a Management Maverick Builds a Brand," *New York Times*, July 23, 2000, http://www.nytimes.com /2000/07/23/business/business-in-china-a-management-maverick -builds-a-brand.html.

9. Yantian and Xuechun, "Haier Rises."

10. Ibid.

11. David J. Lynch, "CEO Pushes Haier as Global Brand," *USA Today*, January 2, 2003, http://usatoday30.usatoday.com/money/markets /world/2003-01-02-zhang_x.htm.

12. Joel Backaler, "Haier: A Chinese Company That Innovates," *Forbes*, June 17, 2010, http://www.forbes.com/sites/china/2010/06 /17/haier-a-chinese-company-that-innovates.

13. Andy Raskin, "When Your Customer Says Jump … By Tailoring His Products to Big Retailers' Every Whim, Michael Jemal Is Teaching China's Largest Appliance Maker How to Build a Billion-Dollar U.S. Brand," *Business 2.0*, October 1, 2003, http:// money.cnn.com/magazines/business2/business2_archive/2003/10 /01/349459/.

14. Ibid.

15. Ruimin, "Raising Haier."

16. "Haier and Higher."

17. Philip Elmer-Dewitt, "At CES: The First Air Conditioner to Carry the Made-for-Apple Logo," *Fortune*, January 8, 2014, http://tech .fortune.cnn.com/2014/01/08/apple-ac-haier-mfi/.

18. Bill Fisher, Umberto Lago, and Fang Liu, *Reinventing Giants, How Chinese Global Competitor Haier Has Changed the Way Big Companies Transform* (San Francisco: Jossey-Bass, 2013), 124.

19. "Haier and Higher."

20. Betsy Morris, "Steve Jobs Speaks Out," *Fortune*, March 2008, http://money.cnn.com/galleries/2008/fortune/0803/gallery.jobsqna .fortune/index.html.

21. Kurt Eichenwald, "Microsoft's Lost Decade," *Vanity Fair*, August 2012, http://www.vanityfair.com/business/2012/08/microsoft-lost-mojo-steve-ballmer. In the quarter ended March 31, 2012, iPhone had sales of $22.7 billion; Microsoft Corporation, $17.4 billion.

22. Walmart, "Our Story," http://corporate.walmart.com/our-story/?povid=P1171-C1093.2766-L6. Revenues for 2013 were $466 billion.

23. Jim Collins, *Good to Great* (New York: HarperBusiness, 2001), 41.

24. "Delta Tops 2013 FORTUNE World's Most Admired Companies Airline Industry List," Delta, February 28, 2013, http://news.delta.com/index.php?s=20295&item=124221.

25. Teresa Amabile and Steven Kramer, *The Progress Principle: Using Small Wins to Ignite Joy, Engagement, and Creativity at Work* (Boston: Harvard Business Review Press, 2011), 81.

26. Steve Blank, "Tesla and Adobe: Why Continuous Deployment May Disappoint Customers," *Inc.*, January 6, 2014, http://www.inc.com/steve-blank/tesla-and-adobe-why-continuous-deployment-may-mean-continuous-customer-disappointment.html.

27. A. G. Lafley and Roger L. Martin, "What P&G Learned from the Diaper Wars," *Fast Company*, February 8, 2013, http://www.fastcompany.com/3005640/what-pg-learned-diaper-wars; excerpted from A. G. Lafley and Roger L. Martin, *Playing to Win: How Strategy Really Works* (Boston: Harvard Business Press Books, 2013).

28. Ibid.

29. Thomas Heinrich and Bob Batchelor, *Kotex, Kleenex, Huggies: Kimberly-Clark and the Consumer Revolution in American Business* (Columbus: Ohio State University Press, 2004), as quoted in Davis Dyer, "Seven Decades of Disposable Diapers," Winthrop Group, August 2005, http://www.edana.org/docs/default-source/default-document-library/seven-decades-of-disposable-diapers.pdf?sfvrsn=2.

30. Ibid.

31. Peter J. Coughlan and Jennifer L. Illes, *Disposable Diaper Industry in 2003*, Harvard Business School case, updated August 5, 2003, Prod. #: 703491-PDF-ENG, available at http://hbr.org/product/disposable-diaper-industry-in-2003/an/703491-PDF-ENG.

Acknowledgments

Thanks to all the clients and Strategic Agility® Think Tank participants who contributed ideas, stories, challenges, and successes. They have provided a great learning environment and valuable feedback. These include Tracy Moore (Acuity Brands); George Sherman (Advance Auto Parts); Matt Rushing (AGCO); Daryl Evans, Glenn Lurie, and Linda Rogers (AT&T); Woody Faulk (Chick-fil-A); John Morrow (Cisco); Celeste Bottorff and Mary-Ann Somers (Coca-Cola Company); Michelle Baker and Steve Necessary (Cox Communications); Wayne Aaron, Jeff Arinder, Ed Bastian, Sandy Gordon, Mike Henny, and Robyn Klein (Delta Air Lines); Chris Baradel, Maria Fernandez, and Michael Griffith (Equifax); Milt Childress, Dale Herold, Steve Macadam, and Ken Walker (EnPro Industries); Ken Calhoon (Forrester); Ron Domanico (HD Supply); Josh Weiss (Hilton); Dana Harmer, Dwaine Kimmet, and Brad Shaw (The Home Depot); Karstin Bodell (IBM); Joel Schellhammer, Bryan Semkuly, and Peter Shipp (Kimberly-Clark); Nelson Chu (Kinetic Ventures); Patrice Miles (Georgia Institute of Technology); Billy Medof (Georgia-Pacific); Hala Moddelmog (Metro Atlanta Chamber, formerly Arby's); Cheryl Bachelder (Popeyes); James Anderson (Turner Broadcasting System); Dean Foust, Ross McCollough, Nancy Nicodemus, and Dan O'Connor (UPS); and Cedric Brown, Jeff Fleck, Tom Moffett, and John Morgan (Zep Inc.). Thank you to Stephanie Tichet of the Connecting Group for introducing me to a fabulous group of innovators, including Andreas Clausen (Beiersdorf), Dane Howard (eBay), Ed Tapan (Google), and Miki Vuckovic (Robert Bosch Tool Corporation).

Too often, we forget to thank the people who have helped to shape our thinking along the way. Thanks to Jim Balloun, who, though he may not realize it, has been a wonderful mentor to me for many years, since we worked together at McKinsey & Company. He was the first to encourage me to write a practical book, one with ideas, processes, and frameworks that companies could put to immediate use. I hope I have succeeded in that. Thanks also to other mentors from my time at McKinsey, including Kevin Coyne, Clem Dougherty, Howard Kaplan, and Rob Yanker, who taught me what a fun, exciting, and rewarding experience consulting can be.

Thanks to my professors at Harvard Business School, especially Robin Cooper, Tom Davenport, Willis Emmons, Elon Kohlberg, Kash Rangan, and Kevin Rock, who opened my eyes to how fascinating business can be, and to Teresa Amabile, who contributed her ideas about how small wins motivate us. Thanks to my students at Emory's Goizueta Business School, and the faculty, including Andrea Hershatter, Susan Hogan, Rob Kazanjian, Patrick Noonan, Jeff Rosensweig, Reshma Shah, and Anand Swaminathan, who gave me great advice on how to help others develop creative and critical thinking.

Thanks to Linda Henman, who identified my passion for helping organizations recognize and capitalize on the changes going on in their marketplaces. Thanks to Henna Inam, for providing expert guidance on how to build a learning community focused on the idea of strategic agility, and to Robbie Baxter, for helping me hone my ideas and develop compelling examples. Thanks to Lisa McLeod for expert guidance and inspiration, to Rose Jonas for early encouragement, and to Bill Lee for his contributions on customer collaboration. Thanks to Christine Carey for organizing a fabulous writers group. Thanks to Andrew Sobel for being a great role model, adviser, and friend. Thanks to Mark Levy, who taught me how to write about what is fascinating to me, and to write in a way that precisely fits who I am. Thanks to Alan Weiss, who provided the perfect advice—always very concisely, and with no kid gloves—at countless junctures, and who connected me with many amazing people in his community.

Thanks to my agent, Giles Anderson, for his enthusiasm and for recognizing how vital the topic of agility is to today's business readers. Thanks to my editors, Karen Murphy, John Maas, Christine Moore, Mary Garrett, and Michele Jones, as well as the rest of the team at Jossey-Bass. I am so appreciative of the care they have taken to make this book something that I can be proud of and that readers will benefit from.

Thanks to Peter Economy, my developmental editor, who has been an invaluable thought partner every step of the way, and has added brilliant finishing touches. He made the process of writing this book fulfilling and fun.

Thanks to my mother, Nancy Keahey, who taught me, by example, how to influence and inspire people, and who pointed me toward excellent company examples for this book. Thanks also to my brother and sister, Calvin Keahey and Julie Keahey, for contributing ideas and perspectives, and to my father, Stan Keahey, who encouraged me to study engineering—which turned out to be the perfect choice—and who taught me to be curious, resourceful, and creative. Thanks to my daughters, Shannon and Alison, who keep me informed about youth culture and technology, and are a delight in every way.

And last but not least, a very special thanks to my husband, Rob, who inspired me, provided countless great ideas, and was invaluable in shaping my message and content. He supported me through many weekends spent writing, and made it possible to fit in great adventures—backpacking, biking, sailing, and skiing—along the way.

About the Author

Amanda Setili is managing partner of the strategy consulting firm Setili & Associates. Organizations like Coca-Cola, Delta Air Lines, The Home Depot, and Walmart hire her to give them unbiased advice about their strategic direction.

Setili has advised organizations in industries as diverse as consumer and industrial products, financial services, technology, nonprofit, and retail. Her work has taken her throughout North America, Europe, and Asia.

Before starting Setili & Associates, she served as director of marketing for Global Food Exchange, consulted for McKinsey & Company (where she planted seeds that became the firm's Kuala Lumpur office), served as chief operating officer of Malaysia's leading Internet services company, and developed products and optimized manufacturing operations for Kimberly-Clark.

Setili served as an adjunct professor at Emory's Goizueta Business School. She earned her degree in chemical engineering from Vanderbilt, and her MBA, with distinction, from Harvard Business School. She is past president and board chair of the Harvard Business School Club of Atlanta.

For more information, please visit www.setiliandassociates .com.

Index

Page numbers in italics refer to figures and tables.